NATIONAL EXTENSION COLLEGE

HISTORY

Approach to

by

Norman Lowe

Nelson and Colne College

NATIONAL EXTENSION COLLEGE
COURSE NUMBER ED24

The National Extension College, 18 Brooklands Avenue, Cambridge CB2 2HN.
Copyright © National Extension College Trust Ltd. 1982.
ISBN 0 86082 328 8

Designer: Peter Hall
Set in 10 pt Press Roman by the National Extension College, Cambridge.
Printed by the National Extension College, Cambridge.

The author

Norman Lowe is Head of History at Nelson and Colne College, a tertiary college in Lancashire. He teaches 'O' and 'A' level History to 16–19 year olds, and has been closely involved in planning and teaching Open College courses.

The Open College was a new concept pioneered in 1976 at Nelson and Colne; it aims to provide adults who may have been out of full-time education for many years, with a second chance of advancing into higher education. The courses were conceived as alternatives to 'A' levels, which in many cases were thought unsuitable for the needs of adults wishing to study on a part-time basis. Open College is now taught in eleven Lancashire colleges which are organised into the Open College Federation of the North West; it has enabled many mature students to go on to University or Colleges of Higher Education.

This introduction to the study of History was part of the original Methods of Enquiry course, a Stage A unit.

Acknowledgements

We are indebted to Professor Arthur Marwick for allowing us to adapt the ideas contained in his Open University booklets, *Introduction to History* (1970) and *The Nature of History* (1970).

We wish to thank Chris Jakes, Assistant Librarian, Cambridgeshire Collection, for his assistance in obtaining the photographs of source material featured in this course.

Illustrations from Chivers' magazines, 1934, 1948 and 1949, © Chivers and Sons Ltd. Permission applied for.

Illustrations of Domesday Book from John Morris (ed.), *Domesday Book* in History from the Sources series, Phillimore, 1981. Permission applied for.

CONTENTS

INTRODUCTION

Nowadays history is reaching a wider public than ever before, largely thanks to television. Impressive series such as 'The Great War', 'The Mighty Continent' and 'Archaeology of the Bible Lands' have drawn on the work of academic historians. The list of such programmes and series continues to grow: in 1981, for example, the BBC was running documentary series on such diverse topics as the allied occupation of Germany after the Second World War and life on a farm in ancient Britain. Dramas based on historical characters — Churchill, Lloyd-George, Henry VIII and Elizabeth I — have caught the imagination; lots of people are finding their curiosity about these subjects aroused and are wanting to know more about history and how it comes to be written. Did all those sensational scenes in the TV series about the Borgias really happen or was it all legend based on gossip?

It seems appropriate, therefore, to take a closer look at history as a study subject. It doesn't matter in the least if you know nothing whatsoever about history: this booklet is not concerned with a particular period in history, but simply with the methods of history. You may be surprised to learn that historians (people who write history) do have special methods of enquiry in the same way that scientists and mathematicians have. In fact, a historian has to follow certain set rules about procedures when he is gathering and interpreting information about the topic he is investigating. He has to be just as rigorous and systematic as a scientist conducting an experiment; no self-respecting historian can afford to write anything which is not supported by the evidence.

Professor Arthur Marwick's Open University booklet, *Introduction to History* (first published 1970) and his longer book, *The Nature of History* (1970) have already examined the historian's methods of enquiry in great detail. But these books are designed for students at University level; for students not yet thinking in terms of University courses, something shorter and more simple is needed. What I have done is shamelessly to borrow and adapt Professor Marwick's approach and many of his ideas (with his permission) to form the basis of Units 1, 2 and 3. These units explain and demonstrate:

- what history is and what is special about it;
- that it is a useful and relevant subject to study;
- what sources of information are available to the historian;
- how the historian, and indeed anybody who wants to be well informed about what is going on in the world around him, must

always question everything he reads and try to assess its reliability.

Units 4, 5 and 6 developed out of my own experiences teaching local history. In these units you will have a chance to use the knowledge acquired in the first three units when you undertake a little research project of your own into a topic of local history. Even an inexperienced student with a limited knowledge of history in general can pursue some genuine research and produce an original piece of work.

The important thing is that you enjoy this booklet; I hope that, if nothing else, it will help to re-awaken your interest in history and arouse your critical awareness of what is being said and written in the world around you.

A note from the Course Editor

The illustrations used in this course have come from Cambridge local history library, the Cambridgeshire Collection. Curiosity prompted me to visit the library after my first reading of the course. How easy would it be for me to find the kinds of material the author described, here on my doorstep? The answer was 'very'. The local history librarian was pleased to hunt out documents for me and answer all my questions. The material fascinated me so much that I decided to include photographs of it in the course to show the results of a first visit to a local history library. I hope it will whet your appetite and set you off on your own research.

UNIT 1
HISTORY AND ITS IMPORTANCE

OBJECTIVES

At the end of this unit you should be able to:
1. distinguish between the three different usages of the word 'history' which are explained in the text;
2. quote arguments to justify the study of history.

MEANINGS OF THE WORD 'HISTORY'

The word 'history' can be used to mean different things. Most people, if asked to give a definition, would probably mention that history had something to do with the past, but you would probably get widely differing answers if you stopped the first dozen people you came across in your nearest shopping precinct and asked them to give you an example of history. You might be unlucky enough to pick on the aggressive type who tells you not to remind him about history, because he hated it at school and couldn't for the life of him remember dates. Some would probably tell you that they absolutely adore history, especially books by Jean Plaidy and Catherine Cookson. Others might mention television series such as 'The Borgias' or Robert Kee's programmes about Ireland. You might even find somebody who happens to have read a serious work of history, such as Allan Bullock's famous biography of Hitler, or Antonia Fraser's equally famous life of Oliver Cromwell; or perhaps *Montaillou*, a book by the French historian Emmanuel Le Roy Ladurie about life in a fourteenth century Pyrenean village.

In fact, basically the word 'history' has two different meanings:
A. everything which has actually happened in the human past, the whole of mankind's past life. It doesn't matter whether any record of it has survived, or even whether any record of it was ever made: if it happened, if somebody said it, or thought it, or did it, or suffered it, then it is history. What happened to your grandfather in the Somme trenches in 1916 is part of history just as the First World War itself is history.
B. man's attempt to describe and reconstruct the past. In other words, what we actually know about the human past. Obviously, the actual past and what we think we know about that past may be two vastly different things. We can only know about it through the work of the person recording it and that of the person writing it (the historian trying to reconstruct the past). If no evidence has survived about a particular part of the past, nothing can be written about it. Unless your grandfather kept a detailed diary of his experiences in the trenches, which might be used by a historian, it is unlikely that he will find his way into history (in its second meaning). Thus, history in the sense of 'what we actually know about the past' is unavoidably incomplete. Some periods and topics have been investigated and reconstructed (whether accurately or not) in great detail, others hardly at all. People often say, for example, that history con-

tains too much about kings, queens, politics and wars, and not enough about 'ordinary people'. The reason for this is, of course, that comparatively few traces of the lives of ordinary people have survived. We can never know the whole truth about the past because it is impossible to write about every single happening.

Arthur Marwick subdivides the second category of history into two, depending on how systematic the attempt to reconstruct the past has been. 'In far-off centuries many writers, poets, singers, made some effort to reconstruct the past, but often without any very positive attempts to distinguish between fact and myth.' As recently as the early part of the nineteenth century writers were often careless about their sources of information, and presented as fact information which was based on legend, or gossip or hearsay. It was only during the course of the nineteenth century that history developed as a scholarly discipline in which the historian began to follow 'certain definite rules of establishing fact, interpreting evidence and dealing with source material'. The German historian, Leopold von Ranke (1795-1886), was one of the first to insist that writers of history should always include references and footnotes giving their sources of information. It was largely thanks to Ranke that history gained acceptance as a respectable subject worthy of being studied at Universities.

Historians nowadays tend to make the distinction between *scholarly history* (which Marwick calls type C history) and what they call *popular history* (type B).

At the simplest level we can say that:

1. *scholarly history* includes books and articles which contain a good deal of information discovered by the author himself from primary sources, and not simply taken from other books. Examples are Sir Lewis Namier's *Structure of Politics during the Reign of George III*, G. R. Elton's *Tudor Revolution in Government* and all the articles which appear in learned periodicals such as *The English Historical Review* and *History*. In every case the author has something new to say about the subject which he has discovered himself from primary sources.

2. *popular history* is history which has been put together using only material taken from other books and not from original documents. Often such books are written primarily for entertainment and information purposes with a wide public in mind, and not with the intention of shedding any new light on the

subject. Their aim is simply to communicate history to as wide a public as possible – certainly an excellent idea, though some academic historians tend to sneer at the popular writers. Good examples of popular history are Arthur Bryant's series on the history of England: *The Years of Endurance 1793-1802, Years of Victory 1802-1812* and many others; and Leonard Cottrell's books about ancient civilisations (*The Bull of Minos, Life under the Pharoahs, The Tiger of Ch'in*). John Prebble's books on Scotland (*Glencoe, The Highland Clearances, The High Girders*) can be put into the category of popular history, because his style is designed to appeal to the layman, though in fact he often makes use of primary sources (for a full explanation of this term *see* Unit 3, p. 29). Serious television documentaries such as Robert Kee's programmes about Ireland make excellent popular history.

You can usually tell which category a book fits into by looking at the reading list or list of sources which the author includes. If he has used any primary sources, the book is quite likely to be scholarly history; if he lists only other books and articles, then it contains nothing original, and can be said to be popular history.

A problem with scholarly history is that often it seems not meant to appeal to a wide audience, since much of it, especially the articles in the learned journals, is scarcely what you would call sparkling reading. Gordon Connell-Smith and Howell Lloyd,[1] two historians working at Hull University, recently launched an attack on historians who persist in writing in such a way, deliberately cutting themselves off from a wider audience in order to keep history a specialised subject for the favoured few academics. They argue that historians are failing in their duty if they do not communicate with a wide public; there should be no reason why type C history cannot be both scholarly and readable at the same time. Many writers have demonstrated that this is indeed possible: Allan Bullock (*Hitler*), E. P. Thompson (*The Making of the English Working Classes*), Antonia Fraser (*Cromwell; Mary Queen of Scots*), Hugh Thomas (*The Spanish Civil War; Cuba: the Pursuit of Freedom*), Emmanuel le Roy Ladurie (*Montaillou*), Thomas Packenham (*The Boer War*) and many others have had books published in paperback, reaching a wide public.

[1] Gordon Connell-Smith and Howell Lloyd, *The Relevance of History*, p. 59.

To summarise, Marwick's three meanings of the word 'history' are:

A. the complete human past;
B. man's attempt throughout the centuries to describe and reconstruct the past;
C. the historian's attempt to reconstruct the past in a systematic and scholarly way, including only information that can be supported by his source material.

SELF ASSESSMENT QUESTION

Usages of the word 'history'

Listed below are some sentences involving the three different usages of the word 'history'. Indicate, by placing A, B or C at the end of each sentence, which meaning you think the author had in mind. You may put two letters if you feel that two meanings are involved. The As should be obvious, but it is not always possible to distinguish clearly between B and C.

Here are two examples to help you:

(a) Our grandfathers and great-grandfathers had a hand in the making of history.   **A**

    This obviously refers to history as the past, since not all our grandfathers and great-grandfathers actually wrote history, though some of them might have done.

(b) More history is being written today than ever before.   **B or C**

    This is probably true of both types of attempt to reconstruct — both popular and scholarly.

Now consider these sentences:

1. *Leopold von Ranke played an important part in getting history accepted at Universities.*
2. *Not everybody would agree that the course of history is determined by great men.*
3. *She always liked history at primary school.*
4. *History is a tragedy in which we are all involved.*
5. *History is too much concerned with the detailed pursuit of trivialities.*

6. *History is a pack of tricks we play on the dead. (Voltaire)*
7. *Nowadays there is plenty of history on television.*
8. *Men make their own history but they do not know that they are making it. (Marx)*
9. *History fulfils a social need.*
10. *The justification for history is that it enables us to see ourselves in perspective.*

SPECIMEN ANSWERS

1. C;   2. A;   3. B, possibly C;   4. A;   5. C;   6. B, possibly C;   7. B, possibly C;   8. A;   9. B or C;   10. B or C

Comments

The important distinction is between A (history as the complete human past) on the one hand and B and C (history as an attempted reconstruction of the past, whether scholarly or not) on the other. If you have *not* put A for (2), (4) and (8), or if you *have* put A for any of the others, study the following explanations, then go back and read through the section again. It doesn't matter too much if you have confused B and C in the others.

Statement (2) obviously refers to the past as it happened, and not to a written attempt to reconstruct the past. Statements (4) and (8) are fairly similar to each other, both referring to the past. The writer of (4), in a gloomy mood, could not have meant B or C, since we are not all involved in writing history. Marx cannot have meant to imply that we are all writers of history, or presumably we would know that we were writing it. Both writers want to convey the meaning that all of us, however small and insignificant, play a part in the whole panorama of history. Whatever it is we do, it immediately becomes part of the past, and therefore part of history.

Statement (1) must be C rather than B because history at University level is a scholarly discipline; (3) would depend upon the type of history taught, but is perhaps more likely to be B, since one wouldn't expect primary school history to be especially scholarly. In (5) the phrase 'concerned with' gives the clue — the past doesn't concern itself with anything; only the historian can be concerned. So it could be B, but I would suggest that the writer probably meant C, because this is the kind of criticism that many non-historians level against what they consider to be the absurdities of minute research, especially in PhD theses. One eminent scientist called it 'crawling upon the frontiers of knowledge with a magnifying glass'. It is probably what Henry Ford had in mind when he made his famous remark about history being bunk.

Statement (6) sees Voltaire in one of his more cynical moods and is probably B, since he clearly hasn't a very high opinion of historians. You could argue that history as an academic discipline would be far too respectable to deliberately play tricks on the dead: and anyway C hadn't been invented when Voltaire (1694-1788) wrote this sentence. Statements (7), (9) and (10) could all be either B or C, though (7) is more likely to be B, since there is probably more of what one might call non-academic history on TV than there is of the scholarly type.

WHY DO WE STUDY HISTORY?

Now that we know what is meant by the word 'history', we ought to devote a little time to thinking about why historians bother to study and write history. There are always plenty of people who feel hostile towards history, for different reasons; sociologists are sometimes critical of historians for their lack of precision; those who were badly taught at school may feel that history is boring; some scientists think that in this technological age, far too much time and money are being wasted on a useless study. And not only scientists: a colleague of mine who taught modern languages used to argue that though history was certainly fascinating (and he read a lot of it himself), it wasn't really any use; according to him I would be better employed teaching French, which would at least be useful to people going on holiday to France. So why do we do it?

1. My modern languages colleague himself provided what must surely be one important justification: it is a good thing to study the past for its own sake, simply because it can be interesting and enjoyable. It doesn't matter whether it can make any contribution to the present or not.

2. Going beyond mere enjoyment, it is possible to argue that historians fulfil a necessary social function in that a good many people want to place themselves in relation to their own past. Marwick makes the point well: 'History is to the community when memory is to the individual.' A society without history is like a man who has lost his memory. We are surrounded by the past — the great cathedrals and castles, the ruined monasteries, the canals and the abandoned railway lines. Anybody with a normal share of alertness must surely feel some curiosity about them. What is the story behind the building of the Leeds-Liverpool Canal, for example? Why does the keep of Rochester Castle have one round tower and three square ones instead of four square ones like most other Norman keeps? Why is Fountains Abbey in its present delapidated state, without a roof and with grass growing all over it? History provides the answers.

3. History gives us a better understanding of the problems of the world today, and therefore helps us to solve those problems. How can we possibly begin to understand the situations in Northern Ireland or Afghanistan, the Arab-Israeli conflict or the Cold War, without studying their backgrounds in history?

4. Some historians would argue that in a limited way a study of history can enable us to make some broad predictions about the future. Although history never repeats itself in exact detail, nevertheless similar situations do arise which often have similar results. For example, every empire from the Egyptian, through the Roman, Spanish and Portuguese to the British, has eventually collapsed. Thus the historian can predict that what we now call the Russian Empire — Soviet control of Eastern Europe — will disintegrate sooner or later; though he can't tell you with any certainty when.

5. The study of history is an intellectual exercise, a good way to train the mind. Of course other subjects can claim the same function, and another colleague of mine argues that learning Latin is the best way to train the mind. But certainly history does practise us in organising and presenting arguments systematically. G. R. Elton in his book *The Practice of History*, claims that 'its real value as a social activity lies in the training it provides, and the standards it sets'.

6. History teaches us about human behaviour, about people in relation to other people, and about how people have reacted to

certain circumstances. As A. L. Rowse puts it: 'With history you have so much more range of experience to draw upon – in fact the whole range of human experience that we know of.'[2]

7. History teaches us to be critical and sceptical of what we read. We shall see later that a historian always has to be on the look-out for whether or not the information he is using is reliable; for example, autobiographies have to be treated with suspicion, in case the author has some personal axe to grind.

8. History is justified simply as the search for truth. It tries to re-construct the past as fully as possible, and so make its contribution along with other studies such as sociology, physics, chemistry, biology and so on, towards building up a complete picture of man's environment. In other words, anything which furthers the extent of human knowledge is justified.

This would seem to be quite an impressive list; one hopes it would be enough to convince the doubters though probably they would not accept some of the points. Historians themselves disagree strongly about their relative importance, and it would be too much to ask you to place them in what you consider to be the order of importance.

ASSIGNMENT A, PART I

However, it would be a good idea for you to consider the above list for a few minutes to see what your reactions are and then pick out what *you think* is the best justification and the one which seems to be the least convincing. Then explain in a couple of short paragraphs the reasons for your choice.

Aim to spend about 20 minutes on this exercise; the idea is to see what your immediate reactions are. And remember there is no definitely right or wrong answer.

Keep your answer and send it to your tutor when you have completed your short piece of work for Assignment A, Part II at the end of Unit 2.

---

[2] A. L. Rowse, *The Use of History*, p. 14.

16

UNIT 2
HISTORICAL WRITING

OBJECTIVE

At the end of this unit you should be able to recognise historical writing as opposed to other types of writing, such as sociology, political science, economics, historical novels.

THE SPECIAL QUALITIES OF HISTORY

One of the controversies that some academics like to argue about is where the dividing line occurs between history and subjects like sociology, economics, anthropology and political science (politics), which are usually classed as the social sciences. We said in our definition that history is an attempt to reconstruct what people have done in the past. But the social sciences also deal to some extent with what people did in the past. Works of literature may also be based on or deal with actual historical events. So what are we looking for in a piece of writing which will enable us to say that it is 'historical' writing?

Normally a piece of historical writing contains three special qualities. It is concerned with:

1. events involving people in the past;
2. a sequence of events, changes or developments which have taken place, together with *an explanation* of *why they happened* and *why they were important*;
3. particular events rather than generalisations.

To expand further:

1. History investigates events involving people in the past. A zoologist writing about prehistoric animals and an astronomer writing about the formation of galaxies are both dealing with the past, but not with the human past; so they are not writing history. It is debatable whether an archaeologist is a historian or not because he tends to be describing states of things; for example, Housesteads Fort on Hadrian's Wall. But the nature of his evidence makes it difficult for him to describe events except in the barest outline. However, archaeology is a form of historical study because it is all part of the attempt to reconstruct the past.
2. History deals with sequences of events or sometimes the ways in which things have changed and developed over a period of time. The 'things' might be institutions, forms of government, particular countries, methods of farming, transport, the living standards of the working class, and so on. For example, there was a series of events in which Napoleon Bonaparte was transformed from an obscure corporal into Emperor of the French and then into an exile on the island of St Helena. Thus the historian, to put it simply, is telling a story — *a narrative*. But more than that: he is trying to explain why that sequence of events happened in

the way it did and with what results; he is, in fact, *explaining and analysing*. Good historical writing, then, usually contains a narrative describing some events, combined with an explanation and an analysis of what caused the events and what effects they had, i.e. why they were important. Sometimes historians write about a state of affairs or a situation in history; this is not exactly a narrative, but more of *a description*. For example, *Montaillou*, by the French historian Emmanuel Le Roy Ladurie, is a detailed account of life in a fourteenth century Pyrenean village. However, the author does not simply describe; he explains and analyses the reasons why life in Montaillou took the form it did.

This business of explanation and analysis is important; imagine a narrative which contained no element of explanation whatsoever and was simply a list of events with dates. The *Anglo-Saxon Chronicle* is a good illustration of this. It was started as a list of important events and was later developed by King Alfred (871-899) into a fuller narrative of each year's events:

949   In this year Anlaf Cuaran came to Northumbria.

956   In this year Archbishop Wulfstan passed away.

959   In this year King Eadwig passed away and was succeeded
      by Edgar, his brother.

This is clearly a crucially important source that the historian can use in his attempt to reconstruct Anglo-Saxon history, but is not in itself a piece of historical writing. It simply records events with no attempt at interpretation. This is what historians call a chronicle.

It is the explanation and analysis part of it which causes the archaeologist some trouble, because although he will be able to describe, say, the two different states of a Roman villa before and after a disastrous fire, he will probably be a bit short of information on the fire itself. Between them, though, the archaeologist and the historian will perhaps be able to arrive at a more complete picture.

3. The historian writes about particular events in an exact sort of way, rather than dealing with generalisations. For example, he might write in a very exact and detailed way about the system of government in France under Napoleon I or in Germany under Hitler, whereas a political scientist might tend to write in broader terms, comparing systems of government in general. The historian may well go on to make statements about how Napoleon's or Hitler's system fits into the general pattern, but his main concern will be to focus on a particular system in as much detail as possible. The political scientist will no doubt make references to specific examples, but his main concern is to look out for general patterns in types of government.

SELF ASSESSMENT QUESTION

Listed below are five passages, some of which illustrate the three special qualities of history:
- events involving people in the past;
- explanations of events, changes and developments;
- particular events rather than generalisations.

Some are not historical writing at all.

For each passage, decide whether you think it is a piece of true historical writing, and write a brief note in explanation (not more than 40 words for each) of your decision. For those passages which are not history, mention what type of writing you think it is. Remember that, to be history, the passage must contain all three special qualities.

Be strong-willed and try to work out the answers before looking at the suggestions. Allow yourself about three-quarters of an hour for this.

Here are two examples which should help you:

The Thirty Years' War was rather a series of struggles than a continuous conflict, which circumstances outside the control of the combatants served to prolong. There were a number of occasions when the logic of events should have made the end of the war probable: but time and time again French diplomacy made the conclusion of peace impossible. From its very start the war promised to be a European rather than a German struggle. It was never confined to a single locality. It flared up all over Europe, now in the Low Countries, now at sea, now in the Lombard Plain or in the Valtelline Valley, now in Saxony and the Rhineland. Its ubiquitous character only makes the war the more difficult to unravel. Yet it is probably true that the intervention of Catholic France and Protestant Sweden against the Hapsburgs was to prove the most vital event in its history.

Specimen answer: historical writing: includes all three qualities — particular events involving people in the past (Thirty Years' War) and some explanation (why the war was so prolonged). (The passage is taken from a well-known history text book — *Renaissance and Reformation* by V. H. H. Green.)

2. Another criticism of the Spartan constitution turns on the indulgence permitted to women. This hinders Sparta from attaining either the purpose of its own constitution or the happiness of its citizen body. Just as husband and wife are alike essential parts of the family, so a state should also be considered as almost equally composed of men and women members. In all constitutions, therefore, where the position of women is poorly regulated, one-half of the citizen body must be considered as left untouched by the laws. 6. This is what has actually happened at Sparta. The legislator who made the Spartan code intended to make the whole citizen body hardy; but if he fulfilled that intention, as he obviously did, in regard to the men, he has wholly neglected to achieve it in regard to the women, who indulge in all sorts of licence and live a luxurious life. 7. The inevitable result, in such a constitution, is the worship of wealth, especially if — as happens with most military and martial stocks — the citizens are dominated by their wives. (But the Celts are an exception to this general rule: so, too, are such peoples as openly approve of homosexual attachments.)

Specimen answer: not history; mention of Sparta in particular, with some explanations; but no sense of narrative and author uses present tense, showing that he is writing *about his own time, not (to him) the past*. (The passage is taken from Aristotle's *Politics* and must be classed as a work of political science.)

Here are your five passages:

Extract 1
    The publication of the Charter was followed by a nation-wide movement to support a national petition for the Charter, and groups and soci-

eties were formed up and down the country. This somewhat haphazard proceeding exposed the heterogeneous composition of the movement which was to prove its fatal weakness. The Chartists included co-operative societies holding the views of Robert Owen, currency reformers, factory reformers, law reformers like Feargus O'Connor, the owner of the Leeds newspaper, the *Morning Star*, disgruntled trade unionists, and Parliamentary reformers. They all met on common ground in detestation of the Poor Law Amendment Act, and disappointment at the limited franchise reforms of the Reform Bill.

The Commons debated the petition, and rejected it by 235 votes to 47. After much argument and talk of action and force, the movement split. The 'moral force' wing withdrew, and the 'physical force' section soon found that their wish to use force was likely to be suicidal. One small but tragic incident showed this clearly. In November, 1839, at Newport, Monmouthshire, the miners organised a march on the town, hoping to give a lead to others. The whole thing misfired, and the leaders were sentenced to transportation. This marked the end of physical-force Chartism, but the whole series of events still further weakened the Melbourne Government.

Extract 2

Perhaps one explanation why there has been so little interest shown in the systematic study of urbanism in this country is that, for emotional and ideological reasons, a traditional anti-urban attitude has developed. It is as though, as a society, we have tried to delude ourselves into believing that urbanism does not exist simply by ignoring it and refusing to come to terms with it. During the period of rapid urbanisation in the nineteenth century, no effort was made to control or direct the expansion of the cities and towns, and the results of this laissez-faire growth were both ugly and unhealthy. The conditions in the urban areas were so bad that they promoted social disorder and chaos. All that was least desirable in society was nurtured in these places, which were generally nothing better than overgrown slums. Large cities were seen as the centres of social disorder and the breeding-grounds of dissension and rebellion. As the dislike of the cities intensified, those who were able to do so moved to the outskirts, and many areas were neglected and left to decay as a result. In the course of time, the outskirts became further removed from the centres of these industrial cities until they began to merge with each other, causing vast conurbations to develop. At the same time, the 'nastiness' of cities was emphasised, and their reputation was seen to be one that was deserved.

Extract 3

Before the industrial revolution, the representative firm was tiny by modern standards, and was owned and managed by one man or by a partnership. The chief industries were carried on on a small scale in the fields or in the cottages, rather than on a large scale in factory and mine. It was only in foreign trade that there was much scope for the large firm. It was in foreign trade, therefore, that the need for large-scale borrowing first made itself felt; and it was in foreign trade that modern methods of finance (e.g. through the joint-stock company) were first evolved.

The channels into which savings could flow, or through which they could be borrowed, were narrow. The landowners and the merchants had almost a monopoly of capital and used it on their land and property or in their businesses without much recourse to borrowing. There was little scope for expansion and little incentive, therefore, to accumulate capital or to borrow it. Improvements to property, social display, and mere extravagance swallowed up what the capitalists of later centuries, putting money before magnificence, would have sunk in stocks and shares, or factory buildings and plant.

Extract 4

Luck and disunity of his opponents will account for much of Hitler's success — as it will of Napoleon's — but not for all. He began with few advantages, a man without a name and without support other than that which he acquired for himself, not even a citizen of the country he aspired to rule. To achieve what he did Hitler needed — and possessed — talents out of the ordinary which in sum amounted to political genius, however evil its fruits.

His abilities have been sufficiently described in the preceding pages: his mastery of the irrational factors in politics, his insight into the weaknesses of his opponents, his gift for simplification, his sense of timing, his willingness to take risks. An opportunist entirely without principle, he showed both consistency and an astonishing power of will in pursuing his aims. Cynical and calculating in the exploitation of his histrionic gifts, he retained an unshaken belief in his historic role and in himself as a creature of destiny.

The fact that his career ended in failure, and that his defeat was preeminently due to his own mistakes, does not by itself detract from Hitler's claim to greatness. The flaw lies deeper. For these remarkable powers, were combined with an ugly and strident egotism, a moral and intellectual cretinism. The passions which ruled Hitler's mind were ignoble: hatred, resentment, the lust to dominate, and, where he could not dominate, to destroy. His career did not exalt but debased the human condition, and his twelve years' dictatorship was barren of all ideas save one — the further extension of his own power and that of the nation with which he had identified himself.

Even powers he conceived of in the crudest terms: an endless vista of military road, S.S. garrisons, and concentration camps to sustain the rule of the Aryan 'master race' over the degraded subject peoples of his new empire in the east.

Extract 5

In the period when these first marine invertebrates were evolving, between 600 and 1000 million years ago, erosion of the continents was producing great expanses of mud and sand on the sea bed around the continental margins. This environment must have contained abundant food in the form of organic detritus falling from the waters above. It also offered concealment and protection for any creature that lived within it. The flatworm shape, however, is not suited to burrowing. A tubular form is much more effective and eventually worms with such a shape appeared. Some became active burrowers, tunnelling through the mud in search of food particles. Others lived half-buried with their mouthparts above the sediment. Cilia around their mouths created a current of water and from it they filtered their food.

Some of these creatures lived in a protective tube. In time, the shape of the top of this was modified into a collar with slits in it. This improved the flow of water over the tentacles. Further modification and mineralisation eventually produced two flat protective shells. These were the first brachiopods. One of them, named Lingulella, gave rise to a line of descendants that still live today, virtually unchanged; they are what are often called living fossils.

SPECIMEN ANSWERS

Extract 1: historical writing: it includes people and particular events in the past with explanations of why the Chartists were protesting. (The passage is taken from *The Victorian Age* by R. J. Evans.)

Extract 2: not history: author is writing about the past and there is some explanation; but not particular or specific enough for history — he only writes about cities in general. (The passage is taken from a textbook on sociology.)

Extract 3: not history: there is reference to the past, but very little explanation; seems to be concerned with firms and capital rather than with particular events in the past. (The passage is taken from a textbook on economics.)

Extract 4: historical writing: the author is writing about a particular person in the past with explanations of his successes and failures.

(The passage is taken from Allan Bullock's famous biography of Hitler.)

Extract 5: not history: author is certainly writing about the past, but not the human past. (The passage is taken from David Attenborough's *Life on Earth*, and is therefore natural history.)

Comments
The important thing about the above exercise is that you spotted (1) and (4) as historical writing, because they display the three special features of such writing. You may well have realised that (2) (3) and (5), are not history, without being able to say exactly what kind of writing they are. The important thing to notice about (2) and (3) is the way in which they demonstrate the close ties that exist between history and other subjects, such as sociology and economics; in addition, political sciences, geography, religious studies and literature all make use of history, usually to provide specific examples of general surveys that they might be making. For example, the economist author of passage (3), writing about how capitalists before the industrial revolution spent money on improvements to their own property instead of investing in factories, goes on to take an example from history: the Earl of Bedford spent £100,000 draining the fens.

We could argue, therefore, that this is *another justification for the study of history:* that it provides social scientists and others with information and material which would not otherwise be available. However, most historians would be unhappy at the notion that history was merely a subordinate subject to the social sciences.

ASSIGNMENT A, PART II

HISTORY AND YOU

For the final exercise in this unit you have a chance to write a short piece of history yourself (about one side of A4 paper). What you have to do is to think of a particular event or set of events which happened during your own lifetime and then explain how these events affected your own life, in other words, why they were important to you. Here are some examples:

The event itself might be one of *great historical importance:*
- *Second World War* — might have resulted in your being severely wounded, widowed, orphaned or evacuated from London or from another city to the country, so that your whole future was changed.
- *Hungarian uprising crushed by Russians (1956)* — might have destroyed your faith in Communism and changed your political outlook.
- *Conservative victory in 1979 General Election* — you might feel that this was a direct cause of the recession which led you to become redundant.

OR It might be an event of only *local importance:*
- *closure of a railway line* — might have caused you to change your habits and life-style;
- *opening of a new super-store* — might have changed your shopping habits or caused your own business to fail.

OR It might be an event of *importance only to you and your family:*
- *an accident* of some sort which left you seriously crippled;
- *a chance meeting* which opened up completely new possibilities for your future;
- *a religious conversion* — perhaps you became a Mormon or a Born-Again Christian, changing your entire approach to life.

These examples should give you some ideas. If you are genuinely unable to think of any event which has affected your life, we shall have to allow you to invent something (though no true historian would ever stoop to such a thing!).

You may refer to books or newspapers for specific dates or details if necessary, but your main concern should be not to write an account of the Second World War, or of whatever event you choose, but to analyse and explain how the events affected you and why they were important to you. You will be writing about *your own experiences*.

Remember to keep in mind *the three special qualities of history:* you will be writing about particular events involving people in the past (your own past) and you will be offering explanation and analysis, in this case of why and how the events were important to you. If you are successful you will have produced a short but genuine piece of your own personal history.

Send your work to your tutor, together with your answer to Part I of this assignment.

UNIT 3
THE HISTORIAN'S SOURCES OF INFORMATION

OBJECTIVES

By the end of this unit you should be able to:
1. distinguish between primary and secondary sources;
2. demonstrate an awareness of the types of primary source material which the historian is able to use in his attempt to reconstruct the past;
3. recognise signs of unreliability or bias in primary sources;
4. recognise signs of bias in historical writing.

WHERE DOES THE HISTORIAN LOOK FOR HIS INFORMATION?

In the first two units we looked at why we study history and attempt to reconstruct the past, and we discussed the special qualities of historical writing which set it aside from other subjects. We are now going to move on to have a look at how the writer of history, the historian, goes about putting together his book, his article or his television documentary. Where does he get his information from to produce his particular bit of history?

His first job is to make sure that he reads what has already been written about his subject. Even if no book has been written specifically on that subject, he would be very foolish if he started ploughing through archives and documents before seeing what information he could find from other books and what useful clues he might find to other sources of information.

To take an example: in the mid 1960s the German historian, Joachim Fest, decided to write a biography of Hitler, though there were already several in existence, including an excellent one by the British historian, Allan Bullock. To begin with Mr Fest had to read these biographies to find out what sources of information their authors had used. If he had merely wanted to produce a book quickly, he could have lumped together all the best bits from the existing books without bothering to look at the source material himself. But this would have added nothing to what was already known about Hitler, and Fest was keen to shed some new light on his background and career. This could only be done if Fest examined for himself the great mass of documentary and other evidence which had come into existence during the Hitler period or soon afterwards; only then could he make his own assessment of Hitler. The sources available included documents about German foreign policy captured from the German foreign office at the end of the war, letters exchanged by Hitler and Mussolini, newspaper reports, newsreel films and recordings of Hitler's speeches, reports of the trials of the war criminals at Nuremberg, and so on. Much information was provided by countless published memoirs and diaries of people involved in the events of the Hitler period such as Otto Strasser's *Hitler and I* (published in London in 1940), William L. Shirer's *Berlin Diary* (London, 1941) and the *Goebbels Diaries* (London, 1949). Fest was also able to use new material which had only recently come to light such as the *Martin Bormann letters* and the *Ribbentrop Memoirs*; these had not been available when Bullock was writing his book (first published in 1952).[1]

Not surprisingly in view of the vast amount of material available, it took Fest almost ten years from his first plans to the finished product, which was published in Germany in 1973 (English translation, 1974). Both books (Bullock and Fest) have been widely acclaimed because of their lack of bias and the thoroughness of their research.

You may be surprised to come across the word 'research' in connection with history; some people associate the word more with science and think of chemists or physicists researching with masses of test tubes. But it is quite permissible to apply it to the historian's work. If we say a historian is researching into a topic it means that he is carrying out a systematic and scholarly investigation of all the available sources of information, and these include some sources which were written or made at the time the events happened, and some sources which were written later by other historians. Very often a historian engaged on research will discover new information not previously known, or will shed some new light on a topic, as Joachim Fest did. This is the sort of history which we described as type C in the first unit.

PRIMARY AND SECONDARY SOURCES

This brings us to the important distinction between the two different types of sources.

1. Primary sources
These are sources of information which were written or made during the period which the historian is investigating. For Joachim Fest the primary sources were the captured German documents, the letters, diaries and memoirs, the newspaper reports and newsreels. Even though some of the diaries and memoirs were not actually published until some years after Hitler's death (*Ribbentrop Memoirs*, 1954, for instance) they are still primary sources because they are concerned

---

[1] The appearance of new material prompted Bullock to revise completely the first edition. He also re-read much of the other documentary evidence which he had already studied, in case he had missed anything important. The revised edition came out in 1964. This is a good example of how difficult it is for a historian to produce a book that will remain the final word on a subject for all time. New evidence is constantly appearing; old evidence needs to be examined again to see if light can be shed on some new facet of the topic.

with events through which the authors lived or in which they were involved; in fact they are writing about their own first-hand, primary experiences. Similarly, the Nuremberg Trials reports are a primary source because they provide first-hand information about events in the Hitler period.

Other examples of primary sources are Samuel Pepys' *Diary* and the *Anglo-Saxon Chronicle*.

Don't be confused by the fact that most of the sources I have mentioned have been published in book form. That doesn't matter: if they are first-hand accounts which came into existence at the time the events they are concerned with actually happened or very soon afterwards, then they are primary sources whether they are still in manuscript form or book form.

2. Secondary sources

These are sources of information written later by historians, about events in the past. One of Fest's main secondary sources was the Bullock biography; and when it was finished, Fest's own book became a secondary source which will be of great use to future historians, as well as being a fascinating account for the general reader.

SELF ASSESSMENT QUESTION

You now have a chance to test yourself to see if you can distinguish between primary and secondary sources. Below is a list which includes both types, taken from different periods in history. In the box provided put a 'P' against the primary sources and an 'S' for secondary. Most are straightforward, but one or two are tricky. To help you here are a couple of examples:

1. *G. A. Craig,* Germany 1866-1945 *, first published 1978*   Ⓢ

   Secondary source − it is a modern book about events which took place in Germany during an earlier period.

2. The Diaries of Field-Marshal Lord Alanbrooke, 1939-46.   Ⓟ

   A day-by-day account of events in the Second World War written by the Chief of the Imperial General Staff − an excellent example of a primary source.

Here is your list:

1. *A. J. P. Taylor*, English History, 1914 to 1945 *(first published 1963)* ☐

2. Acts of the Privy Council of England, 1542-1628. ☐

3. *J. Haynes*, A View of the Present State of the Clothing Trade in England *(published 1706)*. ☐

4. *Sir Winston Churchill*, Marlborough: His Life and Times *(first published 1933/4)*. ☐

5. *Dr Rogers*, Reminiscences of a Workhouse Medical Officer *(first published 1889)*. ☐

6. Household and Farm Accounts of the Shuttleworths of Gawthorpe Hall. ☐

7. *Lord Hailes (ed.)*, The Secret Correspondence of Sir Robert Cecil with James VI *(first published 1766)*. ☐

8. *R. S. Rait*, Five Stuart Princesses *(first published 1908)*. ☐

9. *Sir Walter Raleigh*, History of the World *(first published 1624)*. ☐

10. *Sir Winston Churchill*, History of the Second World War *(first published 1948)*. ☐

SPECIMEN ANSWERS

1. S;   2. P;   3. P;   4. S;   5. P;   6. P;   7. P;   8. S;
9. S;   10. P.

Comments

Most of these should be straightforward. The Ps are the first-hand accounts, written at the time the events they are concerned with actually happened. Also of course, a primary source may have been written later by a person involved in the events.

Publication (7) may be a bit confusing. This is a selection of letters exchanged by James VI and Sir Robert Cecil during the early years of the seventeenth century, and published under the editorship of Lord Hailes in 1776, over 150 years after they were written. But the letters themselves are nevertheless a primary source for a study of the early seventeenth century.

You might have suspected that (9) is a primary source since it was published in the early seventeenth century, but as Raleigh was writing about events that happened long before his own time, it must rank as a secondary source. In fact, he died before he had completed the history as far as his own times.

Publication (10) is the most difficult to classify. This is Churchill writing about events through which he lived and in which he himself played an important role. Much of the book is based on his own first-hand experiences, which would suggest that it is a primary source. On the other hand, it also contains information which Churchill himself collected from other primary sources and which he interpreted in his own way: to that extent it is a secondary source. But in the end we have to say that because Churchill himself was so closely bound up with so many of the events of his book, the whole thing must be regarded as a primary source.

A CLOSER LOOK AT PRIMARY SOURCES

We have mentioned previously, in passing, half a dozen or so types of primary source. But there are far more than these. Here is a fuller list to give you some idea of the enormous range of material which has survived. They are arranged loosely into groups:

1.   Government and other 'official' documents
Royal charters (such as Magna Carta)
Acts of Parliament
Acts of the Privy Council
Royal Commission Reports
White Papers
Surveys (such as Domesday Book)
Census returns
Cabinet records
Diplomatic dispatches
Ambassadors' reports
Manorial records
Local Government records
Parish registers
Poor relief records

Police reports
Legal cases
Port Books (customs accounts)
School minute books

2. Private sources

Estate accounts and records (*The Household and Farm Accounts of The Shuttleworths of Gawthorpe and Smithills* are a well-known Lancashire collection which have been published)

Monastic records (some Whalley Abbey records have been published)

Mill and factory accounts and reports

Wage returns

Reports and minute books of local institutions such as Fire Brigades, Ambulance Associations, Co-operative Societies, Operatic Societies, Cricket Clubs and so on

Trade Union reports and minute books

Letters and diaries

Contracts

Wills and inventories

Many of these sources in groups (1) and (2) such as Acts of Parliament and Royal Commission Reports have been published, as have many parish registers and collections of wills and inventories. Others such as Port Books and many of the local account and minute books will be available only in manuscript form.

3. Printed sources

Parliamentary debates (Hansard)
Newspapers, periodicals and magazines
Memoirs and autobiographies
Pamphlets, broadsheets, manifestos, posters and advertisements.

4. Archaeology

Inscriptions
Remains of forts, villas, walls, burial mounds, etc.
Pots and other articles (coins)

5. Industrial archaeology

Remains of factories

Old machinery

Houses of workers

Canals and railways (remains). Some first-rate collections are being developed, notably the huge open-air folk museum at Beamish (near Durham).

6. Miscellaneous

Place names

Maps

Films, newsreels, records of speeches, photographs

Oral traditions

Personal reminiscences (tape-recorded interviews)

Novels, poems, paintings, sculpture, architecture, which came into existence during the period being studied

And even now there are probably some that I have missed.

Where does one look for sources?

The Public Record Office and the British Museum in London have many of these documents. Stately homes and country houses have often kept their own family collections. Chatsworth, for example, still houses all the Devonshire family records and papers. Every county has its own Record Office for local documents. Many cities have local history libraries and even quite small town libraries have local collections. Of course the County Record Offices would like as many documents as possible centralised in their archives, but local libraries tend to guard their collections jealously.

Between them these primary sources can provide a great wealth of information. To take a few examples: the *Domesday Book* was a survey organised by William I (the Conqueror) to find out about the wealth of the country he had just taken over in 1066. He certainly wasn't thinking about helping future historians, but as it happens the survey gives historians all sorts of information about how society was organised in eleventh century England. Legal cases are useful for studying both the state of law and order and problems of commercial transactions. Port Books are invaluable for a study of British overseas

Blacksmith's, dating from 1550; exterior view

Remains of carpet-beating factory, 1900; exterior view

£500.
REWARD.

WHEREAS several well-known suspicious looking characters, are seen lurking in Bene't Street, and are frequently seen to go into the Eagle; we hope the inhabitants will keep a sharp look out; what their intentions are we know not, they are several in number, and from their appearance are strangers. The principle (as we suppose) is a man of weak appearance, rather tall, with very servile *Manners*, supposed to be drawn into the affair against his inclination—another is shorter, rather sandy whiskers, active, wears a stiff collar round his neck, as he is supposed to be the loudest *Barker* in the gang---another, grey hair, short, surly looking man, deals very largely in *bone manure*, his appearance is that of a madman; another, an elderly man, *Bull*-faced, a very suspicious character, one of the disgraceful *Borough rats*, deals largely in hides, he is tall and stout, awkward made, rather peppery, with a very surly appearance---another is a powerful man, often strolling about Ditton, once very respectable, and a man *Trustworthy*, but supposed to be seduced by the opinions of a titled **Pensioner** residing in the west of the county, concerned in the hateful traffic of Boroughs, of which he fears to be deprived.

Information has been given to the principal officers of the Town to apprehend any of the aforesaid suspicious characters, seen lurking in the Streets or about the County, who shall, upon conviction, receive the above reward, by applying to the Independent Association.

WILSON, PRINTER, JORDAN'S YARD.

Miscellaneous poster

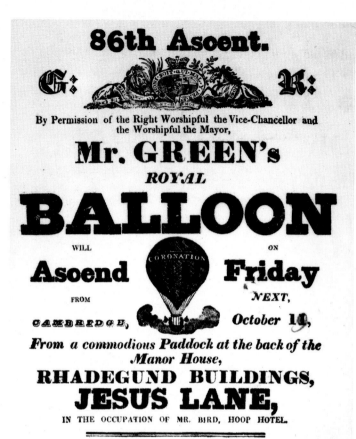

86th Ascent.

G:R:

By Permission of the Right Worshipful the Vice-Chancellor and
the Worshipful the Mayor,

Mr. GREEN's

ROYAL

BALLOON

WILL   ON

Ascend   Friday

FROM   *NEXT,*

CAMBRIDGE,   *October 14,*

From a commodious Paddock at the back of the *Manor House,*

RHADEGUND BUILDINGS,
JESUS LANE,

IN THE OCCUPATION OF MR. BIRD, HOOP HOTEL.

MR. C. GREEN

Who had (by order of Government) the honour to make his first
ascent at his Majesty's Coronation, respectfully announces to the
Nobility, Gentry, and Public, that he purposes making his EIGHTY
SIXTH ÆRIAL VOYAGE.

Tickets of Admission to witness the process of Inflation, attaching
the Car, and launching the Balloon, 2s. 6d. each; to be had at the
Chronicle and Independent Press Offices; and at the principal Inns
and Booksellers in the Town.—Children and Schools will be ad-
mitted at half price.

This splendid Balloon is the same with which Mr. GREEN performed his Nocturnal Ascents from the Royal Gardens, Vauxhall, London. It is composed of 1200 yards of the richest Silk, in alternate
colours of crimson and gold, measures 110 feet in circumference,
contains 141,364 gallons, and with the Car attached, is 60 feet high.

N. B. ENTRANCE OPPOSITE JESUS-COLLEGE.

HATFIELD, PRINTER, CAMBRIDGE.

Poster

TO THE
Gentlemen, Clergy,
AND
FREEHOLDERS
Of the COUNTY of
CAMBRIDGE
AND
ISLE of ELY.

GENTLEMEN,

A numerous and most respectable body of the Freeholders having, in a manner the most flattering, invited me again to become a Candidate for the distinguished honour of Representing you in Parliament, I feel myself in duty bound to obey the call.

After a connection of twenty-eight years, my general principles must be too well known to you to require any explanation.

On the all-engrossing question, which led to the dissolution of the late Parliament, I must candidly avow myself opposed to a measure so wild and sweeping, so fraught with danger to all our Institutions and to the best interests of the Country, more especially the Agricultural Interest, as the Bill lately proposed by His Majesty's Ministers. At the same time, whatever may hitherto have been my sentiments as to the expediency of altering the present Representative System, I shall be ready, in accordance with the general voice of the Country, to concur in supporting any safe and Constitutional measure of reform.

I have the honour to be,

Gentlemen,

Your faithful and obedient Servant,

Charles Somerset Manners.

CAMBRIDGE, *April 28, 1831.*

Election poster, 1831

TO THE INHABITANTS

OF

CAMBRIDGE.

FELLOW TOWNSMEN,

HEARING that a report prejudicial to my character is in circulation, namely, that I sold the body of FRANCIS PORTER, and further that it was without the knowledge or consent of the Overseers:

I beg to state in reply to the first part of the charge, that the body was not sold for any sum, but given up (under a recent Act of Parliament) for examination, with the understanding that the Funeral Expenses should be paid to relieve the Parish, and that he should have Christian Burial at Trinity Church, and might be seen by the Parishioners previous to interment:

To the second part, that of the Overseers not knowing it, they all knew it, and with the exception of MR. SMITH, gave me their consent, and that I only acted as their servant, without the least expectation or understanding of fee or reward.

S. KNOWLES,

Vestry Clerk, Trinity Parish.

(Signed) WM. EADEN,
WM. SMITH, } *Overseers.*
J. P. TWISS,

Miscellaneous poster

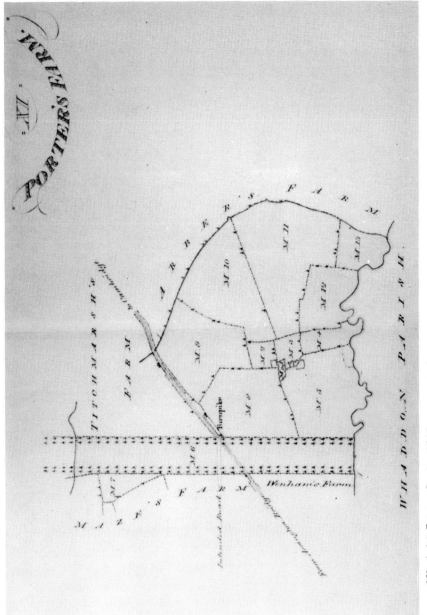

Survey of Hardwick Estates, Cambs., 1815

No. XI. REFERENCE.

Number on the Map	Names of Tenants and Parcels	Quantities
		A R P
	Bird Porter	
	In Wimpole	
M 1	Homestead _ _ _ _ _	_ 3 39
2	Home Close _ _ _ _ _	2 0 19
3	Upper Milking Close _ _ _	1 3 36
4	Lower Ditto _ _ _	3 2 30
5	River Field _ _ _ _	18 0 24
6	Lower part of the Avenue _	31 0 4
7	West of Ditto _ _	3 1 19
8	Sheepwalk Field _ _ _	16 1 3
9	Maldwins Pasture _ _ _	16 3 0
10	Great Ditto _ _	18 3 6
11	Great Pasture (part of) _	26 2 16
12	Ditto (remainder) _	9 0 34
13	Little Meadow _ _ _	5 2 18
		154 2 8

Survey of Hardwick Estates, Cambs., 1815

LIST OF PAUPERS chargeable during the Half-year ended at Lady Day, 1903.

OUT-DOOR RELIEF.

An asterisk prefixed to the name indicates that the Pauper has received medical extras on account of illness of himself or herself or family. In many cases the amount of weekly relief has been augmented or reduced during the half-year in accordance with the varying circumstances of the case ; this frequently occurs where the family is numerous. Where the Pauper is still (end of half-year) on the list the weekly amount is stated, where that is omitted the relief has ceased.

FIRST DISTRICT.

Relieving Officer : C. W. BEAUMONT.

Age of Male.	Name.	Age of Female.	Place of Abode.	Cause of Relief.	Amount received in Half-year. £ s. d.	Present weekly Relief. s. d.
	Adams, Cecilia	73	1, Gentle's yard, Northampton street	Infirmity	4 12 4	3 6
94	Allen, Charles	72	70, Fitzroy street	Infirmity	3 16 2	3 6
	Allensby, Elizabeth	76	1, Miller's passage	Infirmity	3 19 4	3 0
	Arnold, Jane	79	3, Britannia place	Infirmity	3 5 0	2 6
37	Allies, William	37	8, Gloucester place F.S.	Illness of man	2 9 4	
41	Arnold, Frederick		3, Britannia place	Illness	Medical only.	
	Brand, Alice	48	4, Trinity place	Widow, 3 children	1 19 0	1 6
	Brittain, Eliza	66	5, Paradise place	Infirmity	4 6 10	3 6
	Butler, Harriet	70	Merton passage	Infirmity	4 11 8	3 6
35	Butler, Walter S.	30	9, Gloucester terrace	Crippled	3 13 6	3 6
	Buttress, Sarah	72	3, James cottages	Infirmity	4 12 4	3 6
*72	Barber, William	58	4, Albion row	Illness of man	0 12 2	
*	Brown, Elizabeth	44	4, Paradise place	Illness	0 9 6	
*46	Billings, Thomas	46	10, Burleigh place	Illness of wife	0 1 4	
	Beavis, Ethel E.	18	29, Wellington street	Illness	Medical only.	
	Brown, Lily	23	4, Paradise place	Illness	Medical only.	
	Brown, Elizabeth	29	4, Nelson street	Illness of illeg. child	Medical only.	
21	Ball, Arthur		16, Nine Pin court	Illness	Medical only.	
	Bell, Emma	18	13, Burleigh place	Illness	Medical only.	
	Casebolt, Sarah	82	49, City road	Infirmity	0 10 6	
68	Clark, William L.	70	6, Mason's court	Phthisis	7 16 0	6 0
	Clements, Ann	70	4, St. Andrew's court	Infirmity	4 11 0	3 6
84	Coulson, Thomas		6, Porcher's yard	Infirmity	3 19 4	3 0
	Charter, Esther	77	16, Gloucester street	Infirmity	1 18 6	3 6
*63	Chapman, David	60	1, Chiddenton's hill	Infirmity	0 14 4	2 6

Poor relief, 1903

The Minutes of the proceedings of the previous meeting of the Council were confirmed.

The Mayor informed the Council that he had received a letter from Professor Maitland with reference to the freedom of the Borough agreed to be conferred on him, and read the following extract from the letter :—

"I hope that you will be so kind as to let the Borough Council know that I am delighted by the great honour it has done me, and shall be very proud of my freedom. I can say in all sincerity that I feel more than repaid for anything that I have done for the history of Cambridge."

The Mayor stated that on the occasion of the Memorial Service to the late Queen held at the Guildhall by the various Nonconformist bodies in the Borough, they had decided from the subscriptions given at the service to offer to present to the Corporation a Bible which could be kept in the Guildhall, and used for religious services, and he had accepted the Bible on behalf of the Corporation, and expressed his thanks to the subscribers.

Orders were made for payment of various sums of money out of the Borough Fund amounting to £1937 17s. 3d.

The sum of £560 was ordered to be paid into the Borough Fund Wages Suspense Account.

An order was made for payment of £500 to Messrs. Kerridge & Shaw, being the seventh instalment on account of their Contract for the Police Station.

It was reported that £14 12s. 10d. had been paid on account of Criminal Prosecutions in accordance with the regulations made by the Council on the 15th June, 1899.

The payment of £573 15s. 10d. out of the Borough Fund for Police and other wages from the 5th of January, 1901, to the 9th of February, 1901, was reported.

Orders were made for payment of various sums of money out of the District Fund amounting to £2329 18s. 3d.

The sum of £780 was ordered to be paid into the District Fund Wage Suspense Account.

An order was made for the payment of £1013 out of the Infectious Diseases Hospital Loan Account.

An order was made for the payment of £500 to Messrs. Kerridge & Shaw, being a second instalment on their Contract for the Fire Station.

Resolved that the usual authority be given to the Treasurer to honour Cheques drawn by the Borough Accountant for the payment of claims not included in the list approved.

The payment of £858 3s. 8d. out of the District Fund for wages and weekly salaries from the 5th of January, 1901, to the 9th February, 1901, was reported.

Council minutes, 1901

Latin

In Grantesete ten̅ Robt̅. II. hid. *In WEDERLAI Hd̅.*
7 III. uirg. Tra. e̅. IIII. car̅. In dn̅io. I. hida. 7 ibi sunt II. car̅. Ibi XXII.
cot̅. 7 I. molin de XL. sol. De dim̅ Gorth dim̅ mill

Anguill. In tot ual 7 ualuit. VII. lib̅. T.R.E. x. lib̅.
Hanc tra̅ tenuef. IIII. sochi. Hoy un̅ ho̅ Algari com.
tenuit. III. uirg. 7 alij hoes Wallef com. tenuef. II. hid.
7 dare 7 uende tras suas potuef. *In STOV HD̅.*

In Gamelingei. ten̅. II. hoes. I. hid de Robto.
Tra. e̅. I. car̅. 7 ibi est. cu̅. III. cot̅. pr̅u. I. car̅. Nem
ad sepes. Val 7 ualuit. xx. sol. T.R.E. XL. sol. Hanc
tra̅ tenuit. I. ho̅ Algari. 7 uende potuit. *In CESEÞ*

In Draitone ten̅ Auefgot de Robto. III. hid *HD̅.*
Tra. e̅. III. car̅. In dn̅io est una. 7 IIII. uilli cu̅. I. bord
hn̅t. II. car̅. pr̅u. III. car̅. Val. XL. sol. Qd̅o recep. XIII.
sol 7 IIII. den. T.R.E. LX. sol. Hanc tra̅ tenuit Sigar
ho̅ Wallef. 7 potuit recede quo toluit cu̅ saca.

XXXVII TERRA DAVID DE ARGENTOMAGO. *IN STOV HD̅.*

David de Argentomago jn Caldecote ten̅. I. uirg
7 xx. acs. Tra. I. car̅. 7 ibi est cu̅. III. bord. 7 I. cot̅.
pr̅u. I. car̅. Val 7 ualuit. xx. sol. T.R.E. xxx. solid.
Hanc tra̅ tenuit Sigar ho̅ Wallef. 7 recede potuit.

In Crochestone ten̅ Dauid. VI. hid. 7 ibi sunt. II. car̅. 7 IIII. III. pot
7 dim. In dn̅io. III. hide. 7 ibi sunt. II. car̅. 7 IIII. III. pot
fieri. Ibi. VII. uilli. cu̅. VII. bord 7 II. cot̅ hn̅t. III. car̅.
7 adhuc. III. 7 dim po̅s fieri. pr̅u. IX. car̅ 7 dim. Pasta
ad pecun. 7 de herbagio. XVI. den. De Maresch. dp̅ngent

202 a

Translation

In WETHERLEY Hundred
3 In GRANTCHESTER Robert holds 2 hides and 3 virgates. Land for 4 ploughs. In lordship 1 hide; 2 ploughs there.
   4 villagers with 7 smallholders have 2 ploughs.
   22 cottagers;
   1 mill at 40s; from ⅔ weir 500 eels.
   In total, the value is and was £7; before 1066 £10.
   4 Freemen held this land. One of them, Earl Algar's man, held 3 virgates. The others, Earl Waltheof's men, held 2 hides; they could grant and sell their lands.

In LONGSTOW Hundred
4 In GAMLINGAY 2 men hold 1 hide from Robert. Land for 1 plough; it is there, with
   3 cottagers.
   Meadow for 1 plough; wood for fences.
   The value is and was 20s; before 1066, 40s.
   A man of Earl Algar's held this land and could sell.

In CHESTERTON Hundred
5 In (Dry) DRAYTON Asgot holds 3 hides from Robert. Land for 3 ploughs. In lordship 1;
   4 villagers with 1 smallholder have 2 ploughs.
   Meadow for 3 ploughs.
   Value 40s; when acquired 13s 4d; before 1066, 60s.
   Sigar, Earl Waltheof's man, held this land and could withdraw whither he would with the jurisdiction.

37 [39]   LAND OF DAVID OF ARGENTON

In LONGSTOW Hundred
1 David of Argenton holds 1 virgate and 20 acres in CALDECOTE. Land for 1 plough; it is there, with
   3 smallholders; 1 cottager.
   Meadow for 1 plough.
   The value is and was 20s; before 1066, 30s.
   Sigar, Earl Waltheof's man, held this land and could withdraw.

2 In CROXTON David holds 6 hides. Land for 9½ ploughs.
   In lordship 3 hides; 2 ploughs there; a third possible.
   7 villagers with 7 smallholders and 2 cottagers have 3 ploughs;
   a further 3½ possible.
   Meadow for 9½ ploughs; pasture for the livestock; from grazing 16d; from the marsh 500 eels a year.

202 a

Pages showing original text and translation of Domesday Book

A

STATEMENT OF FACTS,

RELATIVE TO THE CONDUCT

OF

The *Reverend* JOHN CLAYTON, Senior,

The *Reverend* JOHN CLAYTON, Junior, and

The *Reverend* WILLIAM CLAYTON:

THE

PROCEEDINGS

ON THE TRIAL OF AN ACTION BROUGHT BY

BENJAMIN FLOWER,

AGAINST

The Reverend *JOHN CLAYTON, Junior,*

FOR

DEFAMATION:

WITH

REMARKS.

PUBLISHED BY THE PLAINTIFF.

THE TIES OF BLOOD SHALL BE FORGOTTEN, THE BONDS OF FRIEND-
SHIP VIOLATED; AND A MAN'S ENEMIES, YEA OFTENTIMES THE
MOST SEVERE AND INVETERATE OF THEM, SHALL BE THOSE OF HIS
OWN FAMILY.
                    Doddridge's Paraphrase on Mat. x. 36.

HARLOW : PRINTED BY B. FLOWER,

FOR E. BUMFORD, NO. 5, NEWGATE STREET, AND
D. EATON, NO. 187, HIGH HOLBORN, LONDON.

1808.

Trial proceedings, B. Flower v J. Clayton, 1808

trade. Letters, diaries and memoirs give a personal, though sometimes biased view of events. Don't forget that newspapers and periodicals are a valuable source on almost any subject you care to mention.

At this point it might prove interesting to take a close look at one particular primary source. Here is a page from *a Chester Port Book for 1565*. These books contain records made by customs officials of ships leaving and entering the port. There were usually separate Inward and Outward Books, detailing merchants, cargoes, captains and destinations. They were started in 1565, and this is a page from the first Outward Chester Book.

It reads:

Undecimo Die Octobris Anno septimo
RRne Elizabreth:

John Middleton and willm Massye of the Cittie of Chester Marchauntes camme into the Custome howsse of our Soveraigne lady the Queene for the port of Chester and hath entredd xviii^C (1800) godes of Manchester Cottons of their owne godes to be transported to Andolozia in the Realme of Spayne in the Bark called the Trinitye of Chester of the bur-   iii^{li}
then of xxvi th Tonnes or theraboutes, wherof willm Davies is master under god, and being conteigned in viii Fardells marked withe their Mark as in the Margene appereth:—

John Middleton

xii^O Die Octobris Anno predicto

Michaell Smythe of the Cittie of Cittie of Chester Marchant likewise doothe enter in the Shipp above named iii^C (300) godes of Manchester   X s
Cottons of his owne goodes and being conteigned in one pack marked with his Mark as in the Margene appiereth.

Mychaell Smyth

xiii^O Die Octobris Anno predicto

Randall leeche of the Cittie of Chester Marchant likewise dothe enter iii^C godes of Manchester Cottons and one of ledd cast of his owne goodes in the Shipp abovenamed called the Trinity of Chester, and   xix ^{s}
being conteigned in ii small Fardells marked withe his Mark as in the Margene appereth.

Randall leech

Books such as this can provide a surprisingly wide range of information:

1. If you study the whole book and then do a bit of elementary mathematics, you can arrive at the total amount of Manchester cottons[2] exported from Chester in 1565, with destinations. You can do the same for other commodities.
2. If you have plenty of time to spare you can look at books for other ports for the same year and try and arrive at the grand total of Manchester cottons exported from England.
3. A look at as many Chester books as possible from 1565 through to 1600 will show how English exports through Chester fluctuated during the reign of Elizabeth I, whether for example there was any increase in cloth exports, or whether there were any slumps; if you study a wide range of books for different ports over the period, you will get indications of general trends in English overseas trade.
4. It is also possible to focus on the careers of particular merchants and follow their progress over a number of years.

A historian wanting to investigate the Lancashire textile industry in the sixteenth century would have to spend a lot of time ploughing through the Port Book volumes. He must also be prepared for disappointment when he tries to build up a complete picture of imports and exports. In fact, so many of the volumes have perished in one way or another (damp, rats, mice, fire) that it is only possible to get tantalising glimpses of what really happened. But at least that is better than nothing.

Other important primary sources for the same subject are legal cases in the Courts of Chancery, Exchequer, Queen's Bench and in the Duchy Court of Lancaster, which give information about the credit procedures involved in buying and selling raw materials and cloth. It is surprising how many people failed to pay up on time or tried to sell defective cloth and found themselves in court as a result.

A third important source is the inventories of weavers and other people connected with the industry which throw light on the life-style of sixteenth century workers. Just as a matter of interest, the Port Books and legal cases are in the Public Record

[2] Cottons were a type of light woollen cloth manufactured in the sixteenth century in the Manchester area and in Bolton, Bury, Rochdale, Blackburn and Great Harwood, though not to any great extent in Colne, Burnley and Paidham which specialised in a heavier type of woollen cloth known as Kersey. This was before the introduction of the famous Lancashire cotton in the early seventeenth century. (gode = goad = 1½ yards.)

Office in London, the inventories are in the Lancashire Record Office in Preston.

HOW RELIABLE ARE PRIMARY SOURCES?

One of the basic lessons a historian has to learn is to be critical and sceptical about primary sources. He must be on his guard against accepting without question everything that a source tells him, since many documents were produced with the intention of deceiving somebody, and the historian has to be wary. Medieval historians, for example, have to be careful when using *charters granting rights to land*. Apparently medieval monks were expert at producing forged charters to supply evidence of rights which they regarded as well established and belonging to their monastery, but which were not founded on genuine deeds.

An ambassador's report to his own government about the situation in the country in which he is stationed may be biased according to his attitude to the nation he finds himself working with. He might be tempted to send his government the kind of information he knows it wants to hear. In the opposite direction, *official government communications to foreign governments* can sometimes be very revealing when compared with instructions given by the same government in secret to its own ambassador about the same situation.

Letters, memoirs and autobiographies are especially suspect; scores of politicians, generals and admirals have produced such works, which, though often excellent reading, are likely to present a biased view of what happened in order to vindicate their own role in the events: Admiral Jellicoe anxious to explain why the Battle of Jutland didn't turn out better than it did in 1916; Napoleon on St Helena blaming the British for not leaving him in peace to finish his work for France; Franz von Papen trying to explain away his role in the appointment of Hitler as German Chancellor in 1933; Sir Anthony Eden defending British intervention in Suez in 1956.

Statistics are another source to be viewed critically: wage and tax returns are obviously suspect; so are official statistics of casualties in battles – the British government tried to minimise their catastrophic losses during the Battle of the Somme in 1916, while the German government vastly exaggerated British losses. Even when no deliberate deceit is intended, one still has to be cautious. It would be wrong, for example, to assume that the trade detailed in the Chester Port Books for 1565 was the total amount of trade through Chester that year; we know from other sources that a substantial amount of smuggling went on, which was obviously not included in the records. Statistics given in newspapers are notoriously unreliable; how often today can we read three different accounts of the same earthquake or flood disaster in three different papers and get three contradictory reports? They were no better in the past. *Newspaper articles* generally have to be treated with caution especially if the paper has some political or religious point of view it is trying to put over.

Legal cases often present unexpected problems when the verdict is not clear or has not survived. A typical example occurred in the Duchy of Lancaster Court in 1587, when the Lancashire aulnager[3] brought a case against a group of Colne clothiers because they had taken woollen cloth over the Lancashire border to Heptonstall in Yorkshire, without having it sealed. In their defence the clothiers claimed that they had not broken the law because the cloth was unfinished; they were taking it to Heptonstall to have it fulled because there was no decent fulling mill in Colne (or so they claimed). The Yorkshire aulnager had inspected and approved the cloth in due course. The problem with this case and with many other sixteenth century court cases is that no record of the outcome of the case has survived. The historian is left trying to decide where the truth lies: were the clothiers trying to pull a fast one or was the Lancashire aulnager only kicking up a fuss because the fee was going into the Yorkshireman's pocket instead of his own?

Sometimes a historian can be completely taken in by a piece of evidence. G. R. Elton (*The Practice of History*) quotes an example of a historian who in 1902 examined the papers of Thomas Cromwell (adviser to Henry VIII during the years 1532-40). He came across two letters which appear to be blackmailing notes from Cromwell to Priors of monasteries allegedly saved from suppression by Cromwell. The conclusion drawn was that Thomas Cromwell must have been a shady character and his reputation suffered. However, G. R. Elton, looking at the original letters, realised that they were written and signed in a hand quite different from that of Cromwell or any of his

---

[3] The aulnager was an official appointed by the Crown; his job was to inspect cloth before it left the county where it had been manufactured. If it came up to the required standards the aulnager or his assistant affixed his seal of approval, for which the clothier had to pay 6d per piece of cloth sealed. It was illegal to take finished cloth out of the county unsealed.

clerks. He concluded that they were really bits of private enterprise by someone hoping to cash in on Cromwell's position and reputation, but the trick was discovered and the letters passed on to Cromwell; they have remained among his papers to this very day. Thanks to Elton, Cromwell's reputation was salvaged, though not until half a century later.

Of course, there is a danger that the historian can be too sceptical and see deviousness in every piece of evidence he looks at, so that he finds it impossible to make any judgement at all. To reassure you, it must be pointed out that there are masses of primary sources which are perfectly straightforward and whose authors had no particular axe to grind.

To sum up: *the historian must make sure that the source he is using is both genuine and reliable.* At this stage it would probably be asking too much of you to decide about the authenticity of sources, but you should certainly be able to have a good shot at detecting signs of bias in a primary source.

SELF ASSESSMENT QUESTION

Primary sources and their problems
Here is a little exercise to see whether you can identify some of the problems with primary sources. Below is a list of problems and weaknesses which historians encounter while trying to interpret primary sources. A primary source which exhibited one of these weaknesses would have to be treated with caution, though the historian would not necessarily have to discount it altogether:
1. *Political bias of the author possibly affecting his judgement.*
2. *Business interests of author and of author's colleagues possibly affecting reliability of his report.*
3. *Author perhaps distorting the truth in order to protect his own reputation.*
4. *Population figures cannot be accepted at face value, because only people who owned land were included.*
5. *Records compiled during a time of great national upheaval are likely to be incomplete.*
6. *Author's dislike of the person he is describing is likely to prejudice his view.*
7. *Memory is not reliable for details after the passage of time.*

8. Relationship between the author and the person described might lead to an exaggeration of the person's virtues.

Here are some extracts from primary sources; each extract has one of the weaknesses mentioned in the list. All you have to do is to decide the weakness of each passage and place the appropriate number from the list in the box at the end of the passage.

For example *if you were faced with an hour's recorded interview with a 98 year old veteran of the Boer War (1899-1902) talking about his experiences at the Battle of Colenso, the weakness of this as a source would obviously be (7).*

Extract 1
A. J. Sylvester (for many years Lloyd-George's secretary) talking about Lloyd George in a television programme

Beginning
'Lloyd-George was the most wonderful, wonderful man I ever knew....'

he continues in the same vein, ending with:
'His speeches used to electrify the House; he was the most brilliant orator ever seen in the Commons.'

Extract 2
Extracts from the Domesday Survey and the Bolden Book, 11th and 12th centuries

(a) *East and West Lulworth, Dorset*
Aiulf himself holds LULVORDE [East and West Lulworth]. Alfred the sheriff held (it) T.R.E. and it paid geld for 8 hides and 3 virgates of land. There is land for 5 ploughs. In demesne there are 3 ploughs and 3 serfs and 3 villeins and 8 bordars with 1 plough. There (are) 12 acres of meadow and 6 furlongs of pasture in length and as much in width. It was worth £6. Now (it is worth) £7.

(b) *Haske, Upton Hellions, Devon*
The bishop [of Coutances] has a manor called CRIDIA [Creedy: probably Haske, Upton Hellions] which Goda held T.R.E., and it paid geld for 1 virgate. This 2 ploughs can till. Drogo holds it of the bishop. There D(rogo) has 4 villeins who have ½ a plough. Worth 5 shillings; when the bishop received it 12 shillings and 6 pence. It belongs to the manor called Morceta [Morchard].

(c)   *Redworth, Durham*

In Redwortha [Redworth] 16 firmars hold 16 bovates, and they render for every 2 bovates 5 shillings and two hens, and for every bovate they do 3 boon-works in the autumn with 1 man and they reap 1 day with 8 men and they cart hay 1 day with 8 carts and they plough one day. Three cottiers hold 12 acres, and in every week every man works from Lammas to Martinmas 2 days in the week and contrariwise 1 day.

Extract 3
From Emmanuel Shinwell's autobiography I've lived through it All

. . . the press revelled in stories of present disaster and imminent catastrophe, reducing the upper and middle classes — and a goodly proportion of those of the working class still in employment — to a state of hysteria.

Even so, the three weeks of alarmist campaigning in 1931, liberally bespattered with venomous attacks on socialism, did not arouse the electorate sufficiently to produce heavy voting. The figure was 76.3 per cent, 0.2 per cent above that for the sedate election of May 1929. The Labour vote dropped to 30.6 per cent, only a little below the familiar figure for the 1920s of about one-third of the total electorate. The critical decrease can be ascribed at least in part to an effective lie invented or spread by Runciman that among the Labour Party's ideas was a plan to rob the Post Office Savings Bank of depositors' money.

As regards seats the Labour Party was virtually annihilated as an effective Opposition. It held fifty-two constituencies . . . I was among the 243 Labour MPs to be defeated.

Extract 4
From the Parish Registers of Parkham, Devon

1644

Burials

Beare. Grace the wife of George Beare	14 Dec.
Pow. Francis Pow the elder	9 Feb.
Pow. Francis Pow the younger	17 Feb.
Wadland. Richard Wadland	4 Mch.
Game. Honor the wife of John Gaine	9 Mch.
Dorks. The waddo woman Dorks	11 Mch.
Galsworthy. Simon Galsworthy	16 Mch.

Marriages

Stanlake, Robert of Woolfardisworthy (husbandman) & Elizabeth Ashton	25 Feb.
Jewell, Valentine (husbandman) & Mary Lee	13 Mch.
Glover, Thomas (husbandman) & Mary Squire	19 Mch.
Jolliffe, Thomas (husbandman) & Elizabeth Brend	26 Mch.
Hedger, William (husbandman) & Susannah Hern	13 Ap.
Shortridge, James (husbandman) & Elizabeth Allin	14 May
Jewell, Hugh of Clovelly (husbandman) & Susanna Nanckivill	23 May

Extract 5
From Sir Anthony Eden's Memoirs, Full Circle

The careless view has been taken that the events of Suez constituted a success for the United Nations. Unhappily this was not so. There is still no known instance of effective action by the United Nations when the two great powers of the world have been in opposition. The United States and Soviet Russia joined together in the General Assembly to issue their instructions on Suez. They were obeyed, but the fact that the United States and Russia were together did not mean that they were right. They could hardly both be so. The Russians are still in Hungary as the Egyptians are in sole command of the canal. . . .

Suez was a short-term emergency operation which succeeded, and an attempt to halt a long-term deterioration, whose outcome is still uncertain. A clash between Israel and Egypt was inevitable, given Nasser's declared intentions. Whenever this took place, it could bring grave danger to the general peace. It was far better that it should not happen at a moment of Egypt's choosing, and the explosion could not have occurred in circumstances less damaging, given the speedy action of Britain and France. On balance the world stood to gain by the fact that the conflict took place then and not some months later, when the consequences in relation to world events might have been infinitely graver.

Extract 6
From Andrew Ure, Philosophy of Manufactures (1835)

. . . I have visited many factories, both in Manchester and in the surrounding districts, during a period of several months, entering the spinning rooms, unexpectedly, and often alone, at different times of the day, and I never saw a single instance of corporal chastisement inflicted on a child, nor indeed did I ever see children in ill-humour. They seemed to be always cheerful and alert, taking pleasure in the light play of their muscles – enjoying the mobility natural to their age. The scene of industry, so far from exciting sad emotions in my mind, was always exhilarating. It was delightful to observe the nimbleness with which they pieced the broken ends, as the mule-carriage began to recede from the fixed roller beam, and to see them at leisure, after a few seconds' exercise of their tiny fingers, to amuse themselves in any attitude they chose, till the stretch and winding-on were once more completed. The work of these lively elves seemed to resemble a sport, in which habit gave them a pleasing dexterity. Conscious of their skill, they were delighted to show it off to any stranger. As to exhaustion by the day's work, they evinced no trace of it on emerging from the mill in the evening; for they immediately began to skip about any neighbouring play-ground, and to commence their little amusements with the same alacrity as boys issuing from a school . . . .

☐

Extract 7
From Beatrice Webb's Diary. *She is writing about A. J. Cook, one of the miners' leaders during the 1926 General Strike.*

He is a loosely built ugly-featured man – looks low-caste – not at all the skilled artisan type, more the agricultural labourer. He is oddly remarkable in appearance because of his excitability of gesture, mobility of expression in his large-lipped mouth, glittering china-blue eyes, set close together in a narrow head with lanky yellow hair – altogether a man you watch with a certain admiring curiosity . . . it is clear that he has no intellect and not much intelligence – he is a quivering mass of emotions, a mediumistic magnetic sort of creature – not without personal attractiveness – an inspired idiot, drunk with his own words, dominated by his own slogans. I doubt whether he even knows what he is going to say or what he has just said.

☐

SPECIMEN ANSWERS

Extract	Weakness
1.	8

Extract	Weakness
2.	4
3.	1
4.	5
5.	3
6.	2
7.	6

You probably managed to work the answers out by a process of elimination: perhaps (4) was the one which was least obvious, but the date should have given you the clue — 1644 was during the English Civil War, certainly a time of national upheaval.

PROBLEMS IN HISTORICAL WRITING

To round off this unit we must look briefly at the end product of the historian's labours, the secondary source which he has produced. Researching and pondering over the evidence can be difficult enough, but many historians find it just as difficult to write up their findings in such a way that other historians and critics will find them acceptable. There is always a lot of argument among historians and disagreement over the interpretation of sources; because of this, history is always being re-written.

Why is there so much controversy among historians?
Here are some of the reasons for you to think about.

1. *The imperfect nature of primary sources;* they may be fragmentary like the Port Books; they may be biased; and different sources may contradict each other.
   Of course, there is unquestionably a large body of knowledge which is agreed on by historians and about which no dispute seems possible. Napoleon lost the Battle of Waterloo in 1815; a battle took place around the River Somme in 1916 with British and French troops fighting Germans; German troops invaded Poland in September, 1939. Without such basic facts as these, it wouldn't be possible to write history.

However, once the historian tries to clothe these simple facts with more details and to ask questions about the facts, he runs into the problems. Why did Napoleon lose the Battle of Waterloo? Was it because his powers of leadership were waning, or because Wellington was a better general, or because the arrival of the Prussians late on in the battle made all the difference? Or was it a combination of all three? The historian has to rely on the sources, and the evidence is not clear-cut. British reports probably tend to concentrate on Wellington's greatness and play down Napoleon's declining powers, while German sources make much of the contribution of Blücher and the Prussians. What the historian has to do is to look at as wide a selection of evidence as possible, including some neutral sources, and then attempt to arrive at the truth. Whatever conclusion he reaches he can be certain that he has not said the final word. Two examples have already been mentioned: G. R. Elton produced a new interpretation of the career of Thomas Cromwell from the same primary source material as was used by earlier historians: and Allan Bullock re-read much of the primary source material before revising his biography of Hitler.

A famous controversy occurred when A. J. P. Taylor wrote his book *Origins of the Second World War*, which first appeared in 1961. Historians had agreed that Hitler was responsible for the outbreak of the war, but Taylor caused something of a sensation in the academic world by seeming to suggest that Hitler was not to blame; according to Taylor, he had not intended a major war, and had been lured into one by the appeasement policies of Chamberlain and the French, which had convinced him that Britain and France would never make a stand against Germany. Taylor had discovered no new evidence: he had reached this vastly different conclusion by *re-interpreting the same evidence* that earlier historians had used to blame the war on Hitler. Several other historians were quick to attack Taylor, accusing him of misusing the evidence; the debate became quite heated, and even now it is not possible to say with certainty which is the correct interpretation. One of the reasons for the disagreement is that much of the evidence for what Hitler intended consists of documents written by German diplomats who may well have covered up some of the more extreme aims of the Nazis. Taylor tends to accept these at face value, while other historians take them as unreliable and attach more importance to Hitler's own statements about his aims in his book *Mein Kampf (My Struggle)*, which mentions a German takeover of Russia.

The complete truth must therefore always remain beyond the reach of the historian.

2. *New evidence is constantly coming to light.* For example, some British official documents such as Cabinet papers are not released until 30 years have elapsed; thus a historian studying recent British history always has to be prepared for a revision of his work. When the Cabinet papers for 1956 are released in 1986, new light will probably be shed on the British government's involvement in the Suez Crisis. Vincent Cronin produced a new biography of Napoleon which probably got closer to the truth about the Emperor than any previous study had done, because he was able to include material from recently discovered sources.

Thomas Packenham challenged a number of widely held views in his book (1979) about the Boer War (1899-1902). It had long been accepted that the war went badly for the British until the Commander-in-Chief, Buller, was dismissed for incompetence. After Kitchener and Roberts took over, the tide turned and the British coasted to an easy victory. Another legend of the war was the brilliant defence of Mafeking by Lord Baden-Powell who defied the Boers and the food shortages until Mafeking was relieved. Packenham discovered lots of new evidence including some Boer sources written in Afrikaans, which had never been studied by a British historian. He showed that Buller, far from being incompetent, was learning fast in a difficult situation, and was beginning to evolve the correct strategy. His replacement by Kitchener and Roberts who were unfamiliar with the situation and were, if anything, less competent than Buller, actually delayed the British victory. Having restored Buller's reputation, Packenham proceeded to dent Baden-Powell's, who, he claims, managed to make the food supplies spin out only by expelling from Mafeking thousands of black Africans, many of whom were slaughtered by the Boers. Baden-Powell called it 'sacrificing the nigger' to save the whites.

Perhaps the most dramatic re-interpretation of all occurred when an American historian claimed to have discovered evidence showing that Joan of Arc was really a man.

3. *Different generations of historians have different views about what are the important themes in history.* As the twentieth century has proceeded, historians have become more interested in what was

happening to ordinary people in the past; so there has been a shift of emphasis from writing as if kings and politicians were all-important towards taking more notice of social and economic matters. A history of the nineteenth century published in 1978 will therefore be quite different from one published in 1920.

4. *Differences of outlook among historians of the same generation:* historians often allow their interpretations to be coloured by their own personal views about such subjects as politics and religion. When this happens, a historian is said to be presenting a subjective (biased) view. All sorts of examples may be quoted: most nineteenth century German historians were notorious for allowing their obsession with German nationalism to distort their writings; a recent Soviet book claiming to be a history of the Second World War, devoted only one short paragraph to the part played by Britain. Sometimes bias can be revealed in a mild sort of way simply by choice of adjective. Thus, a Conservative historian explaining why Labour lost the General Election of 1931 suggests as an important reason 'a well-grounded fear on the part of the working-class elector that his savings were not safe under the control of the Socialists'. If he had omitted the adjective 'well-grounded', the statement would have been objective (showing no bias); the decision to include the adjective reveals his subjective approach.

There used to be a great argument about whether it is possible to write history in a completely objective way, and if it were possible, whether it would be desirable, since such history would very likely make dull reading. The general opinion today seems to be that a certain amount of subjectivity is no bad thing because it stimulates replies from historians with opposite views and the ensuing debate will probably add something to the agreed body of knowledge, even though no final agreement will be reached.

However, the historian must not deliberately set out to prove a case which suits his own prejudices. Unless he gives proper consideration to the opposite viewpoint, he will probably produce bad history.

ASSIGNMENT B

SUBJECTIVITY (BIAS) IN HISTORICAL WRITING

Here are some extracts from historical writings which show varying degrees of subjectivity. Some are more biased than others. After studying each one carefully, write down in what ways the passage seems to be subjective (give examples of phrases or adjectives which reveal bias) and, if possible, say what the obvious subjective influences are, i.e. strong political or religious feelings. You should also comment on whether you feel the writer oversteps the permitted mark to such an extent that he has produced bad history. Aim to write between 40 and 80 words on each passage.

Remember that most historical writing today contains some element of subjectivity; it would be very difficult, if not impossible, for a historian to prevent his own personal view from showing through every now and again, even if only by his choice of adjectives. And this is a good thing because it adds spice to writing and stimulates argument; a piece of writing which was clinically objective all the way through might tend to be boring. Where subjectivity can be criticised is when a writer ignores evidence which does not fit in with his prejudices, or when he wholly condemns someone or some policy without looking at evidence for the defence.

This is a difficult exercise, but the two following examples will help you to see what I mean:

Example 1

In adapting this new power to the satisfaction of its wants England could not escape from the moral atmosphere of the slave trade: the atmosphere in which it was the fashion to think of men as things . . . .

In the early nineteenth century the workers, as a class, were looked upon as so much labour power to be used at the discretion of, and under conditions imposed by, their masters; not as men and women who are entitled to some voice in the arrangements of their life and work . . . .

The needs of the London workhouses on the one hand, and those of the factory on the other, created a situation painfully like the situation in the West Indies. The Spanish employers in America wanted outside labour, because the supply of native labour was deficient in quantity and quality. The new cotton mills placed on streams in solitary districts were in the same case. The inventions had found immense scope for child labour, and in these districts there were only scattered populations. In the workhouses of large towns there was a quantity of child labour available for employment, that was even more powerless and passive in the hands of a master than the stolen negro, brought from his burning home to the hold of a British slave ship. Of these children it could be said, as it was said of the negroes, that their life at best was a hard one, and that their choice was often the choice between one kind of slavery and another. So the new industry which was to give the English people such immense power in the world borrowed at its origin from the methods of the American settlements.

Specimen answer: This writer shows a hostile attitude towards industrialists during the Industrial Revolution. Masters looked upon workers 'as so much labour power. . . not as men and women', and he compares them to slave traders. There is no attempt to defend the employers or to suggest that not *all* employers were bad. Therefore he is perhaps a bit too biased. The passage is taken from W. L. and B Hammond, *The Town Labourer.*

Example 2

The Soviet people cherish the memory of the feats of British and American sailors, who, with the support of the Soviet navy and aircraft, warding off attacks by enemy raiders, submarines and bombers, broke through to the Northern ports of the USSR and delivered military supplies. In the fierce battle for the external communication lines in the Barents and the North seas, Soviet ships and aircraft successfully co-operated with the forces of the Allied British Navy. While the Soviet Union shed its blood in the struggle with the enemy — an enemy threatening all of progressive mankind — the US and British governments had the opportunity to muster their forces, build up an invasion army and strike a blow at the Nazis. The leaders of the USSR understood that the Allies needed a certain amount of time for the mobilisation of these forces. But the Soviet people counted on reciprocal understanding of the need to minimise this time by virtue of the arduous and bloody conflict on the Soviet-German front. During the negotiations among the Allies agreement was reached on the necessity of the creation of a Second Front in Europe in 1942. . . .

With the outset of spring 1942 a precarious military situation confronted the Soviet Union. The fact is that in 1942 there was no other country in the world carrying on such a wide military effort against the Nazis. The Soviet troops fought against the fascist army in what amounted to a one-against-one combat. In this most difficult period of the war the Soviet Union single-handedly carried on the military and economic conflict with the enemy also because the US and British governments, despite their pledges, stymied the opening of a Second Front against Nazi Germany in the West . . . .

In 1943 the Soviet people were once again forced to bear alone the brunt of the fighting against the Nazi forces.

Specimen answer: This passage begins with glowing praise of Britain and the US but the tone gradually changes to one of hostility. He talks of the second front being 'stymied', implying that the western powers deliberately postponed the second front to embarrass the Russians. Obviously sympathetic towards Russia; perhaps a Russian writer? On the other hand, he does give credit to the British and American navies, so it is a more balanced view than the first example. Let's call it a stimulating piece of writing. The passage is taken from K. Gusev and G. Naumov, *U.S.S.R. A Short History*, in fact by two Soviet historians.

Here are your extracts:

Extract 1

Beautiful in person, attractive in manner, able, acute, brilliant even, in intellect, Mary Stuart [Mary Queen of Scots] had many qualities which might have been turned to good account for the welfare of her country. But, brought up in a French court, her moral code was neither of the highest nor the purest; educated under the supervision of her uncles of Lorraine, she was taught to believe that the one great object of her life was to advance the interests of the Roman Catholic Church; and sister-in-law to him whose name is for ever blackened by the massacre of St Bartholomew, she was not likely to be over scrupulous as to the means which she would employ to gain her end.

Extract 2*

In the meantime the Prussian forces had been assembled. Without any declaration of war, without any demand for reparation, in the very act of pouring forth compliments and assurances of good will, Frederick [the Great of Prussia] commenced hostilities. Many thousands of his troops were actually in Silesia before the Queen of Hungary knew that he had set up any claim to any part of her territories. . . . The selfish rapacity of the King of Prussia gave the signal to his neighbours. His example quieted their sense of shame. His success led them to underrate the difficulty of dismembering the Austrian monarchy. The whole world sprang to arms. On the head of Frederick is all the blood which was shed in a war which raged during many years and in every quarter of the globe, the blood of the column of Fontenoy, the blood of the mountaineers who were slaughtered at Culloden. The evils produced by his wickedness were felt in lands where the name of Prussia was unknown.

*I am indebted for extracts (2) and (5) to N. H. Brasher *The Young Historian*, OUP, 1970.

Extract 3

It would be better if World War I and World War II were called the First and Second German Wars: which would define their origin and character, and their place in history. Other nations, before the Germans, had fought wars of aggression and aimed at world dominion; even so it is the ethos of a nation which determines the nature of its wars and dominion: hence again the importance of the German character of the two wars of our generation. The rise of a united Germany completely changed the political physiognomy of Europe and, which may seem singular, the mental and moral physiognomy of the German people. From excessive, and often nonsensical, political fragmentation, Germany passed over to a disciplined, centralised unity, and from unmeasured subjectivism the German gradually passed over to totalitarian Gleichschaltung. But pygmy principalities and the Leviathan State, spiritual anarchy and spiritual regimentation, are opposite expressions of the same political incapacity to build up a sound human community. The political creations of the German are inorganic and grotesque; the work of the typical introvert. . . .

But to what extent is the average German responsible for the misdeeds of his rulers? Attempts to absolve the German people of responsibility even for the Second Reich, the creation of the Hohenzollern kings and the Junkers, are unconvincing in view of the wide and genuine popularity it enjoyed and the devotion it commanded. And as for Hitler and his Third Reich, these arose from the people, indeed from the lower depths of the people, and the unmeasured adulation of which the Fuhrer became the object was as spontaneous as the man was self-made. Friends of the Germans, most appreciative of them as individuals, must ask themselves why individual Germans in non-German surroundings become useful, decent citizens, but in groups, both at home and abroad, are apt to develop tendencies that make them a menace to their fellow-men?

Extract 4

Official Russia during this year (1912) celebrated with unusual pomp and to the peal of bells the tricentennial of the ruling dynasty. It toasted the future of the Romanov House, little suspecting that this was the last such celebration, for tsarist Russia.

Three hundred years earlier the tsarist crown had been placed upon the head of the 16-year-old Mikhail Romanov. One hundred and eight years later this crown had become an Imperial one. On the throne now sat the fifteenth representative of the dynasty – Nicholas II – by the will of God Emperor and autocrat of all Russia, the Tsar of Poland, the Grand Duke of Finland, and so forth, according to the official documents. He had not inherited the mind of Peter I, who had founded the capital of the empire and cut through a "window to Europe". However he did have the cruelty of Nicholas I, for which the great Russian writer Leo Tolstoy had called him "Genghis Khan with a telegraph" and he demonstrated the poverty of intellect characteristic of his father, Alexander III. The last emperor of Russia confessed that the effort to think was so difficult that it could disturb the horse on which he was sitting at the time! Nicholas II and his wife Alexandra Fyodorovna, an imperious woman, both hysterical and superstitious, were the embodiment of the fossilised absolute monarchy and the power of the feudal landowners.

Extract 5*

It is well to pause and look for a moment at this small band of heroes (i.e. the London Protestants who distributed Tyndale's 1526 translation of the Scriptures); for heroes they were, if ever men deserved the name . . . . Such were the first Protestants in the eyes of their superiors. On one side was wealth, rank, dignity, the weight of authority, the majority of numbers, the prestige of centuries; here too were the phantom legions of superstition and cowardice; and here were all the worthier influences so pre-eminently English, which lead wise men to shrink from change, and to cling to things established, so long as one stone of them remains upon another. This was the army of conservatism. Opposed to it were a little band of enthusiasts, armed only with truth and fearlessness; 'weak things of the world,' about to do battle in God's name; and it was to be seen whether God or the world was the stronger. They were armed, I say, with the truth. It was that alone which could have given them victory in so uneven a struggle.

Send your answers to your tutor.

UNIT 4
YOUR VISIT TO THE LIBRARY

OBJECTIVES

By the end of this unit you:
1. will have had some experience of looking at primary sources;
2. will have carried out a preliminary investigation in preparation for your project in Units 5 and 6;
3. will be aware of the sort of information which your chosen primary source example can provide.

IMPORTANT NOTE: If, for whatever reason, you are unable to reach a library which has primary sources, or if you are housebound and can't get to a library at all, it will still be possible for you to do a worthwhile exercise in this unit, and a project in Units 5 and 6. Read the whole of the unit in the usual way, but first turn to p. 57 for your special instructions.

We spent some time in Unit 3 thinking about the many different types of primary sources available to the historian. But no amount of reading about primary sources can arouse the same interest or sense of anticipation as actually browsing through some sources yourself.

The objective of this unit is for you to go to your local library and see for yourself what primary sources they have in their collection. These may be both printed sources and manuscript sources which have not been published. Remember, the important thing which decides whether a source is a primary one is not whether it is printed but whether it came into existence at the time of the events with which it is concerned (*see* Unit 3).

Examples of printed primary sources are:
- Old newspapers
- Statutes of the Realm
- Hansard (the verbatim reports of Parliamentary debates)
- Census returns
- Corporation minutes and by-laws
- Hospital management committee reports

Examples of primary sources which may still be in manuscript form are:
- Diaries and journals (unpublished ones)
- Wills and inventories
- Accounts books and records of local businesses, firms and estates
- Minutes of local organisations and societies
- Parish records
- Vestry minutes

THE THREE TASKS ON YOUR VISIT TO THE LIBRARY

On your visit to the library you have three tasks to complete:

1. The first is to *make a list of eight primary sources – five printed ones and three in manuscript form* (that is, if the library has manuscript documents).

Much depends on how lucky you are with your local library. Large city libraries usually have extensive collections of primary sources, including Statutes of the Realm and Hansard. Some, like Manchester Central Library, have a separate local history library housing their manuscript collections. Here your main problem may well be the overwhelming amount of material available. Smaller libraries are easier to tackle, though some of the smaller ones may not have any primary source material.

Before you go along it is important to contact the head librarian, either by telephoning or writing. A quick phone call will settle the question of whether or not they have any primary sources; if they haven't, they should be able to tell you the nearest library which has a collection. You need to warn the librarian exactly what the object of your visit is so that he is prepared for you when you arrive. This is important, because manuscript collections are kept locked away from public view, so that it will not be possible to complete the exercise without first enlisting the librarian's help.

The vast majority of librarians are pleased to help and eager to show their manuscripts; you might even be lucky enough to find a librarian who will do the whole exercise for you. Often libraries in small towns have interesting manuscripts which local organisations, firms and families have chosen to donate to them rather than to the County Records Office. For example, the library at Colne in Lancashire has a modest but rewarding collection of primary sources, mostly to do with local history. The librarian, Peter Wightman, and his assistant, Mildred Ellis, have prepared a catalogue of local primary sources and an index of items in the local newspaper going back as far as 1874. A student working on this assignment at Colne Library would be particularly lucky.

He might well have chosen his list from the following items:

Primary sources

Printed

Colne and Nelson Times, 1874 to present and *Colne Observer* 1899-1903

Colne Parish Church Magazines from 1897

Census Returns for Colne and district, 1841, 1851 and 1861

Clitheroe Court Rolls, 1425-1567 (3 volumes)

Colne Corporation Acts, 1895-1933

Incorporation of Colne – statistics 1894

Colne Charter Day Celebrations, 14 September 1895 – Official Programme

Hartley Hospital – plans, descriptions, opening ceremony programme, 1924

Railway Acts affecting Colne, 1845-1910
Local celebrations connected with George V (1910-36), 23 pamphlets

Manuscripts
Colne Co-operative Society Minute Books from 1884 (15 volumes)
Diary of Elizabeth Shackleton, 1762-81
Colne School Board Minutes from 1889
Overseers of the Poor Accounts 1767-87
Colne Fire Brigade Reports, 1886-1941
Baptist Church Minutes 1807-44
Colne Copyhold Accounts, 1558-60 (photocopies)
Lancashire Quarter Sessions Papers, 1649-50 and 1749-50 (photocopies)
Colne wills and inventories (1559-1674)
Colne Operatic Society Minutes from 1935

As you compile your two lists, don't just include the first items of each type that you come across: look out for those which attract your interest. *This brings us on to the second task:*

2.   Your visit to the library is not simply to give you a chance to browse through some primary sources. It is also a preliminary investigation in preparation for the climax of the course – your own research project. As you select your eight items, be on the look-out for sources which particularly take your eye and which seem to contain the right sort of information for working up into a project. Documents written before the middle of the seventeenth century may present problems unless you have had some experience of reading early handwriting; but eighteenth and nineteenth century manuscripts should be straightforward enough. Much depends on your personal interests, so it would be a good idea for you to *read carefully through the list of suggested projects on page 61. before you embark on your visit.*

However, it doesn't matter too much on this first visit if you fail to decide on a topic for the project.

3.   Your third job is to choose *one* of the local history sources which has caught your interest, either printed or manuscript, and have a closer look at it. Then make a list of the type of information which it seems to be offering. Try to include at least six points. One

of my students who did this exercise at Colne Library became fascinated with the Colne Fire Brigade Reports, particularly the first volume covering the years 1886-98. This is a manuscript source but it is in good condition and the handwriting is clear and easily legible. This student's six-point list of the type of information provided by this source was:

1. when the brigade was formed;
2. what problems had to be faced with organisation during the early days;
3. how the money was raised to buy the first fire engine;
4. how they performed at their first fire;
5. the most common causes of local fires;
6. whether any firemen were killed or injured.

Instructions for students unable to reach a library which has primary sources

There is no reason why you should not attempt two out of the three tasks; with judicious use of the telephone or post and gentle persuasion of the librarian to do the bulk of the work for you, you can get something interesting and worthwhile out of this unit.

Find out, either by phoning or by writing, whether your nearest library has a primary source collection. If it hasn't, the librarian will be able to tell you where there is one. Having run some primary sources to earth, your plan of campaign should be:

1. Telephone or write to the head librarian, explain exactly what you are doing and ask for help. Ask him or her if it would be possible to make you a sample list of primary sources (5 printed and 3 manuscript – as mentioned on p. 54). It may be possible for them to tell you over the phone without too much trouble or they may prefer to send it by post. In my experience, librarians are delighted to help and feel pleased that someone is showing an interest in their sources.
2. Since you are not able to get to the library, it will not be possible for you to attempt the research project based on primary sources; consequently task (2) (trying to decide on what project to attempt) does not apply to you. However, *the third operation is perfectly possible by means of photocopies.* You would be most unfortunate if your chosen library didn't have a photocopying machine; however, it will be best to make sure at the outset. Careful negotiation with your librarian, probably best conducted

by phone, should make it possible for you to obtain copies of half a dozen or so sheets or pages from one of the primary sources (these probably cost around 10p a sheet).

Some sources lend themselves better to photocopying than others. At Colne library it would be possible to make copies of, for instance, pages from the School Board Minutes, the Fire Brigade Reports and the official programme for the Charter Day Celebrations, among many others. You will have to rely on the good sense of the librarian to choose an interesting source, so it is most important that you explain exactly why you need these photocopies — i.e. to make a six-point list of the type of information provided by this source (*see* p. 56). It might even be possible, with astute manoeuvring and skilful use of the sellotape, to produce a copy of a full newspaper page so that you could have a go at the newspaper advertisement project suggested on p. 60:

ASSIGNMENT C

At the end of this unit, if all has gone well, you should have some or all of the following to send to your tutor:

1. A list of printed primary sources (5 items) and a list of manuscript primary sources (3 items).
2. A list of six points demonstrating the type of information which *one* of these primary sources is offering.

If you visited a library and were fortunate, you will also have:

3. Some ideas about what topic you would like to investigate for your project.

UNIT 5
A LOCAL HISTORY PROJECT

This unit and the next (Unit 6) will give you a reasonable period of time (spread over three weeks) to carry out research and write up your findings about a topic of local history.

OBJECTIVES

By the end of this unit you will have demonstrated your ability to:
1. make effective use of primary sources;
2. integrate information from both primary and secondary sources (though this will depend on which project you chose).

NB If you are unable to reach a library which has primary sources or you are house-bound, your project will have to take a different form. It will be a good idea to read the next few pages, for interest, but your assignment instructions are on p. 65.

RESEARCHING YOUR OWN PROJECT

The climax of the course lies in these two units, 5 and 6, in which the entire time is devoted to a little research project of your own on a local history topic of your own choice. The idea is for you to make use of the knowledge and skills you have acquired connected with primary sources (Unit 3). With a bit of luck you will be able to produce a small piece of genuine research based on one or more primary sources, with perhaps some additional material from a secondary source to put your local information into a wider context. You will have made a contribution towards building up a complete picture of man's past, which is one of the main aims of all historians.

The important thing is not to panic at the prospect of some real 'research', which admittedly does sound rather daunting! In fact, this exercise is very much what you yourself choose to make of it, depending on your interests, the amount of time available and how lucky you are with your library and its sources.

Before you have your panic I want to make one important point which is worth remembering in case you find the other suggestions off-putting: if you are having problems with your library – you can't find a suitable source and nothing seems to be taking your interest – *it is still possible to produce a worthwhile piece of work, simply by using an old newspaper*. Even the most unsatisfactory library should have some copies or microfilms of old newspapers. Choose one issue of a local or national paper, say for the year 1900 for argument's sake, and base your research on this one issue. After reading it through carefully, you should be able to write about:

- what topics were in the news (there will probably be something about the Boer War);
- which topics seemed to be considered of most importance (you will probably find that at this time local papers contained much national and international news);
- how the layout and the style of reporting differ from those of modern newspapers.

One of the most successful projects I have seen was a simple one of this kind. The student chose the earliest surviving issue of the *Colne and Nelson Times* (one for 1875) and found himself idly scanning the adverts. To his surprise he began to find the items advertised, the prices, and the style of the adverts more and more intriguing, and his project almost began to write itself as ideas and comparisons began to occur to him. Eventually he produced an interesting and witty essay of over 1,000 words comparing 1875-style advertising favourably with its modern counterpart. This was a perfectly valid and original piece of research in the sense that his basic raw material was a primary source which nobody else had used.

Having fortified you with the knowledge that if all else fails you can always fall back on the single newspaper type of research, I will give you *some suggestions for slightly more ambitious projects*, all of which have been carried out successfully by Open College students.

Provided your library has similar sources, there is no reason why you shouldn't find at least one of them feasible. The primary sources used are mentioned in brackets:

- A period in the history of a local trade union. Especially good in Lancashire are local branches of the Weavers' Union (Weavers' Union minute books plus information from local newspapers).
- A period in the history of a local Co-operative Society; Colne Co-op minute books, for example, go back to 1884 (Co-op minute books and newspapers).
- A history of a fire brigade (fire brigade reports and newspapers).
- A history of a church (church council minutes, pamphlets, magazines and newspapers). If this subject appeals to you, you may have to visit the vicar, priest or minister for permission to look at minutes. These are usually kept at the church, though some churches have handed them over to the local library.
- A comparison of a village or township at two different times in its history. A highly successful project along these lines was put together about Lomeshaye (Nelson) in 1841 and 1851 based almost entirely on census returns; these should be available for most areas for the years 1851, 1861 and 1871. You could do a simple survey of your area in one of these years, showing details about the population sizes of families and occupations. Or you could compare a limited area in two of the years to find out what changes had occurred.
- A period in the history of a local town or parish council (council minutes and newspaper reports). Parish councils were first set up by the Local Government Act of 1894, sometimes called the Parish Councils Act. If this one appeals to you, it might be a good

idea to find out if any local township took advantage of the Act and set up a parish council.

- A history of the cinema or the theatre in your area (newspapers, programmes, recorded interviews).
- A history of a cricket club or football team (Annual Reports, newspaper reports, minutes of meetings). Your first move would be to contact the club secretary who ought to be able to tell you where the records are kept.
- A history of a local firm (Annual Reports, newspapers, interviews with people who used to work there).
- A period in the history of the local Independent Labour Party (ILP) branch (minute books, newspapers, interviews with early members), or of one of the other political parties.
- A study of a local personality — a teacher, industrialist, musician, actor, writer, suffragette, etc. provided there is no biography already in existence (newspapers, interviews, reviews, minutes, letters).

The problem with some of these topics is that you may well find yourself trying to cover too long a period and end up swamped by masses of information which doesn't seem to fall into any pattern. If this seems to be happening, choose a short period of five or ten years and limit yourself strictly to that. But try to choose a period when something interesting seems to be going on. One student, for example, wrote an excellent project about the first ten years of Colne Fire Brigade, describing the formation of the brigade and all its early problems (such as not having their own engine), and including a graphic account of their first fire. She also looked at a secondary source, a history of fire fighting, and tried to find out how Colne fitted into the national pattern: was it usual for a town of that size to have its own brigade in the 1880s or was Colne setting a trend? Another student investigated the cinema in Nelson in the period 1900-1914.

If this 'period in the history of' approach doesn't appeal to you, another possibility is to focus on one single event. Some successful projects of this type have been:

- The granting of a Charter of Incorporation to a town (newspaper reports, early council minutes, official programmes and brochures). The librarian should be able to tell you if and when your town became a borough and what material they have available.
- An important local strike (newspaper reports and trade union minute books). There were widespread strikes among textile work-

ers, dockers, seamen, miners and transport workers in 1910, 1911 and 1912 which are a good area for investigation. Another good idea might be to try and find out what happened in your town or village during the General Strike — 3-12 May 1926 (newspapers).

- The setting up of a new parliamentary constituency (newspaper reports). Again your librarian should be able to put you on to information about when your local constituency came into existence.
- A General Election in your constituency (newspaper reports, pamphlets, records of the political parties). Many students keen on politics have found this a fascinating area. In case you are interested, I had better point out that there have been General Elections in 1874, 1880, 1885, 1886, 1892, 1895, 1900, 1906, two in 1910, 1918, 1922, 1923, 1924, 1929, 1931, 1935, 1945, 1950, 1951, 1955, 1959 and 1964. Do I need to mention more? There were some before 1874 of course, but you may find that your local newspapers don't go so far back. You can write about the candidates, the campaign, the issues, incidents in the campaign and on polling day. Perhaps there was a bomb scare at the count as there was in the Croydon by-election in 1981. And of course, you can build up the tension before you reveal the result.

One of the most successful of these 'single event' projects examined the setting up of Nelson and Colne as a separate constituency and the first election fought there in 1918. In this case the primary sources were all newspapers which supplied full details of the candidates, programmes, speeches, demonstrations, incidents, and of course, the result. They also provided information about the General Election over the whole country, so that it was possible to see whether Nelson and Colne followed the national trend. In fact it was a huge victory for the Lloyd-George coalition, but the Labour Party managed to increase its representation from 39 to 59. Nelson and Colne returned a Labour MP. A quick look at a secondary source to confirm the general impression would be a great help in this project.

These are just a few ideas for your guidance. You may have thought of something completely different.

ASSIGNMENT D, OPTION I

Your assignment for this unit is to send your tutor your notes and ideas about the project, the sources you are hoping to use, and the headings or sections you expect to write under. This is a most important operation; if you want to avoid your project turning into a shapeless mass of facts you have to try and divide it into sections, each dealing with a different aspect of the topic. You will probably find that the information you collect begins to fall naturally into different categories, and you will be able to give a brief indication or example of what you will write about in each section. Some examples from previous successful projects will show the sort of thing needed at this stage:

Example 1

Project title: The Building of Foulridge Church, 1905 (Foulridge is a village near Colne).

Sources to be used: *Colne and Nelson Times* (in Colne Library); early Foulridge Church Magazines (at the Church); official programmes for the foundation stone laying and the consecration and opening (at the Church); interview with a local resident.

There will be a paragraph (or section) on each of the following:
1. why the villagers decided they needed a new church (Anglicans wanted to rival Methodists who already had a chapel in the village: Church of England was afraid of losing its grip on the working classes);
2. how they raised the cash (donations, bazaars, etc.);
3. laying the foundation stone and the building process (after the ceremony, a thousand people sat down to tea at a shilling a head);
4. consecration and opening ceremony (carried out by Bishop of Manchester);
5. work and popularity of the first vicar (commonly known as 'Ping Pong' because he enjoyed playing table tennis with the young men after the Sunday evening Bible class).

Example 2

Project title: The General Election in Burnley in 1906.

Source to be used: *Burnley Express* (in Burnley Library).

There will be a paragraph or section on each of the following:

1. background to the election — political trend in Burnley since previous general election in 1900 (held by Tories, but marginal seat; socialist support growing);
2. the candidates (short background to each — Conservative, Liberal and Socialist);
3. the campaign (brief summary of main issues — Tories wanted to introduce tariffs, i.e. import duties as cure for unemployment; other two against this because it would increase cost of living);
4. election day (great excitement, brisk polling, socialist, H. M. Hyndman, expected to win);
5. the result (tension at count; narrow Liberal victory — statistics; Hyndman very close third — great improvement on socialist vote in 1900 election);
6. conclusion (Burnley followed national trend — Liberals won general election and Labour increased MPs).

IMPORTANT NOTE: Units 5 and 6, though separate, do in fact together make up one operation and therefore it is important for you to read the comments in Unit 6 before you attempt this assignment.

If you have any problems, put these to your tutor when you send in your assignment.

ASSIGNMENT D, OPTION II

THE ALTERNATIVE PROJECT FOR STUDENTS WITHOUT ACCESS TO PRIMARY SOURCES

As I suggested earlier, the climax of the course is where you indulge in a bit of your own research using at least one primary source. If this is not possible, for whatever reason, you can still do a fascinating and worthwhile exercise using *a selection of current newspapers*; don't forget that today's newspapers are tomorrow's primary sources.

First you have to organise your newsagent to keep for you or deliver copies of five or six different newspapers for the same day: *The Times, Daily Telegraph, The Guardian, Daily Mail, Daily Express, Sun, Daily Mirror* and *Morning Star* (*not* the *Daily Star*) should give you a good cross-section of all types of newspaper. Do try and get hold of the *Morning Star* (which used to be called the *Daily Worker*) which can always be relied on to provide stimulating and controversial opinions.

What you will be doing over Units 5 and 6 is studying these papers carefully, as if you are a historian researching among primary sources. Be on the look-out for contradictions and differences of style and language in the way the papers deal with the same items. You can be pretty certain that whatever day you choose there will be some disagreements and contradictions somewhere. They may not occur in the main news items, so make sure you peruse all parts of the papers – including sports news, editorial comments, and reviews of plays and concerts, where critics are notorious for their differences of opinion.

As you notch up the contradictions, you will begin to get some inkling of the difficulties historians have to face as they try to build up an accurate picture of what really happened. As part of your project in the next unit you will need to concentrate on one topic about which the papers do not agree. *Your assignment for this unit* is to send your tutor a list of four news items in which you have found contradictions or inconsistencies. Mention the papers concerned and a brief reference to the nature of the contradiction.

For example, a list compiled from the papers for Tuesday, 18 May 1982 might look something like this:

1. Falkland Islands Crisis:
    Sun out of step with all other papers – states categorically on front page: 'This is it; Task Force told: Get set to start shooting; get ready to invade.' Typical *Sun* sensationalism. Other papers much more cautious; no mention of orders; e.g. *Mirror* says 'Britain will know this week whether the problem can be resolved by peaceful means.'

2. Ian Botham in car smashes:
    Slight disagreement about what he actually collided with in his first crash

— *Mirror:*	hit a bump, then a fence
— *Sun:*	collided with a post
— *Mail:*	hit a marshall's post

3. Elizabeth Taylor appears on stage in wheelchair after spraining ankle:
    Contradiction about audience reaction
    - *Express:* mentions 'spontaneous applause as she was pushed on stage'. Sympathetic article talking about her bravery and how much pain she was in.
    - *Mail:* 'She turned drama into farce; she had the audience nearly falling off their seats as she made her entrance propelled by the stage manager.' Not at all a sympathetic treatment — making her look ridiculous.

4. Demolition of derelict flats in Liverpool goes wrong and destroys nearby houses as well:
    All sorts of **contradictions**, particularly about how many blocks of flats were **actually** demolished
    - *Times* **mentions** only one; *Guardian* says four; *Express* and *Telegraph* both have five; while *Mail* carefully avoids mentioning the number.

Newspaper of 1885

The Cambridge Observer,
AND COUNTY GUARDIAN.

No. 72.   CAMBRIDGE, JULY 28, 1885.   ONE PENNY.

ANNO VICESIMO SEPTIMO & VICESIMO OCTAVO

VICTORIÆ REGINÆ.

★★★

Cap. ccxl.

An Act for authorizing the *Peterborough, Wisbeach, and Sutton* Railway Company to extend their Line of Railway; and for other Purposes.

[25th *July* 1864.]

WHEREAS by "The *Peterborough, Wisbeach, and Sutton* Railway Act, 1863," the *Peterborough, Wisbeach, and Sutton* Railway Company, in this Act called "the Company," were incorporated, and authorized to make a Railway from near the Town of *Peterborough* to *Thorney, Wisbeach,* and *Sutton :* And whereas by the said Act the Company were authorized to raise a Sum not exceeding One hundred and eighty thousand Pounds in Nine thousand Shares of Twenty Pounds each, and to borrow on Mortgage a Sum not exceeding Sixty thousand Pounds : And whereas it is expedient that the Company be authorized to make and maintain the several new Lines of Railway and Works by this Act authorized : And whereas Plans and Sections of the said intended Railways showing the Lines and Levels thereof, together with a Book of Reference to said Plans containing the Names of the Owners and Lessees, or reputed Owners and Lessees, and Occupiers of the Lands through which the same will pass, have been deposited in the Month of *November* last in the Office of the Clerk of the Peace at

26 & 27 Vict. c. ccxxii.

[*Local.*]   39 *G*   *Wisbeach*

AN

A C T

TO

Authorise the mayor aldermen and burgesses of A.D. 1932.
the borough of Cambridge to acquire lands
for the extension and improvement of the
Guildhall ; to confer further powers upon
the Corporation with regard to certain
recreation grounds commons and open spaces
in the borough and the health local government and improvement thereof; to enlarge
the powers of the Conservators of the River
Cam ; and for other purposes.

[ROYAL ASSENT, 16TH JUNE, 1932.]

Whereas the borough of Cambridge (in this Act called *Preamble.*
" the borough ") is a municipal borough under the
management and local government of the mayor
aldermen and burgesses of the borough (in this Act
5 called " the Corporation ") and the Corporation acting
by the Council are the urban sanitary authority for the
borough :

And whereas the Corporation are the owners of
the Guildhall in the borough and powers for the
10 re-building and altering of the Guildhall were conferred upon them by the Cambridge Corporation Act
1850 :

And whereas it is expedient to authorise the
Corporation to acquire lands for the further alteration

Corporation Act 1932; printed primary source

At a meeting of the Cambridge Book Club Oct 19. 1917

Present President of Queens (Mr Fitzpatrick)
Mr F. M. Clark
Mr Baderach
Dr Wood
Mr Benham
Mr Valentine Richards
D Holland Rose
D Haddon
& Mr Lock (Secy)

It was agreed to excuse Mr Buckland who was not in Cambridge having been held up on his journey from London by an air Raid warning

It was agreed to fine (19)the Master of Corpus (Mr Nairn
D Reid
Mr Wilson
& Professor Stanley Gardiner

It was agreed to elect Mr Cole a member

The President of Queens' College & Mr Wilson having ordered books to the value of 15/6 and 15/- during the year were fined 4/6 and 5/- respectively

Mr Lock was reelected Secretary for the year

A hearty vote of thanks was passed to the President of Queens for officiating as Auctioneer.

[Note An air raid warning was sounded in Cambridge this evening at about 8 P.M. & the meeting was held by the light of candles, the Electric light being very dim.]

Cambridge Florist's Society minutes 1843; manuscript primary source

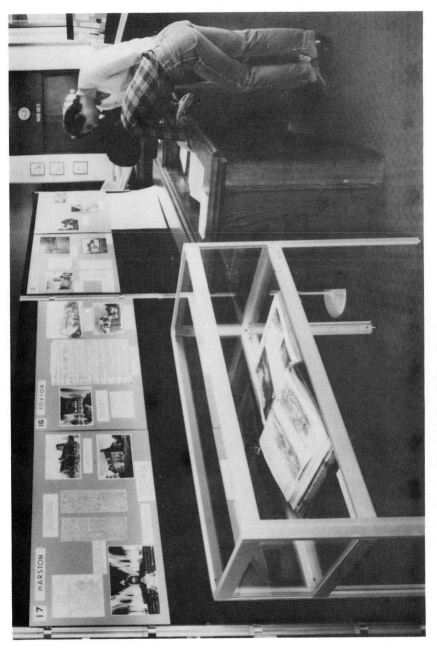

Cambridgeshire Collection displays: Cambridge local history library

BITS OF OLD CAMBRIDGE

No 7   THE FIRE BRIGADE

A humorous view of Cambridge Fire Brigade

FIRE AT TRINTY HALL, CAMBRIDGE.—(SEE PAGE 182.)

An artist's impression of a Cambridge fire

Cambridge fireman, early 1900s.

Fire engine demonstration, Ely, Cambs. 1912

FOUR GOLD MEDALS. FIVE FIRST CLASS DIPLOMAS.

CHIVERS' PURE JAMS

DIRECT FROM THEIR FRUIT FARMS.

AWARDED FIRST PRIZE, ROYAL SHOW, WINDSOR, 1889.

Hospital says :
"The most excellent Strawberry it is possible to buy."

Irish Society says :
"Simply the most perfect ever made."

Woman's Signal says :
"Nothing could be nicer."

CHIVERS'

ORANGE

MARMALADE

UNSURPASSED FOR PURITY AND FLAVOUR.

S. CHIVERS & SONS, HISTON, CAMBRIDGE.

Proprietors of the First Fruit Farm Factory Established in England.

Advertisement for Chivers' jams, 1901

During recent years the suggestion has often been made that the firm should issue a staff magazine. To this idea the Directors have always been favourably inclined, but the production of a really good magazine is no easy job. It requires much time and organisation, especially as a publication of this kind must be made up of items which will be of definite interest to the majority of the firm's employees. The demand for literature in its more popular form is already met by the multitude of magazines on sale nowadays.

This issue is intended mainly to furnish a sort of résumé of those happenings during the year which are likely to be of particular interest. Should it be found desirable and practicable, further issues may appear from time to time.

We hope you will like this effort, and if in your opinion due prominence has not been given to certain events or departments, please forgive us—the cause, in all probability, is scarcity of space rather than any lack of appreciation of values. In future issues the work of other departments will be referred to more fully.

Our special thanks are due to several friends outside the firm who in response to our request have sent us contributions. Building up this ship has been hard, exciting work —we hope it will be a good launch !

Message from the Directors

IT was with great regret that we reached the decision to dispense with the annual teas and entertainments which, with one or two breaks, have been customary in December.

The reasons are probably self-evident. Arrangements for accommodation and transport for a largely increased staff have become more difficult in recent years, and the resulting increase in expenditure is not considered to be justified at a time of difficult business, when all reasonable economies must be effected.

Fortunately the new works magazine will enable the directors' usual annual report to reach every employee, and we welcome its advent for this reason, and also because we hope that it will help to maintain that personal contact which has always been a conspicuous feature of our organisation.

Thanks are due from every section to those who have contributed to the production of this very useful organ, especially to Mr. Muir and his staff who have designed and edited the magazine at a time when the Advertising Department is sufficiently hard pressed with its ordinary duties.

THE PENSION FUND

By the time this message is printed, the first annual accounts of the Pension Fund will have been issued, and they show what a large responsibility we have all undertaken in the establishment of this scheme.

During the year sixty four members of the staff have retired and are now in receipt of a pension from the fund, and while we regret that they have reached the retiring age, it is a great consolation to us

Chivers' first staff magazine, 1934

BAGS OF PEAS AT HUNTINGDON
Above A CHIVERS FARM AT MONTROSE
Centre A HISTON 'PT CLASS
Centre PICKING 'VICS IN AUGUST

THE ORCHARD FACTORY
HISTON CAMBRIDGE

CHIVERS MAGAZINE
CHRISTMAS 1948

Cover of Chivers' magazine, 1948

Page from Chivers' magazine, 1949

UNIT 6
WRITING UP YOUR PROJECT

OBJECTIVE

By the end of this unit you will have demonstrated your ability to communicate your findings from primary and secondary sources in a piece of orderly historical writing involving the main elements of such writing discussed in Unit 2.

ASSIGNMENT E, OPTION I

Your job now is to fill out your plan into the final version of the project, making use of any suggestions or advice received from your tutor. As you prepare to launch yourself into the real thing, you need to keep the following points in mind:

1. You are only writing a fairly short project, so as you collect your information, pick out and make notes only about what seem to be the key points, and then try and communicate these simply and clearly. For example, the writer of the Burnley election project, wanting to include a brief introduction to the candidates (*see* p. 65), was faced with a whole column in the *Burnley Express* about Hyndman, the socialist candidate. But, in fact, for her purposes only three or four main points needed to be made; this could be done in the following way:

> Although Hyndman came from a wealthy background and had been educated at Eton, he was attracted to Marxism, and had Founded the Social Democrat Federation in 1881. He had been trying for several years to get into parliament and had already fought Burnley unsuccessfully in 1895.

Approach each section in this way, mentioning the important facts, but keeping on the look-out for the occasional colourful detail, how, for instance, some people in Burnley even decorated their dogs with party colours and rosettes on election day.

2. *How long should the project be?* This depends entirely on you – on how much time you have available, how much time you are prepared to spend, how much information you have discovered. As a minimum, aim for 600-700 words, or roughly two sides of A4 paper. At this length the Burnley election project with its six sections would fall into six paragraphs of only just over 100 words each. This shouldn't be too daunting for you – even the little piece about Hyndman works out at 46 words. You can give each section its own heading. Here is an actual section, made up of a single paragraph, taken from the election project:

> *Election Day*
> The day began with a heavy shower of hail which was repeated several times during the morning. Polling was quiet until the mills stopped at

11.30 a.m. and then there was a run on the 18 polling booths. Carriages and motor cars sped about the town crammed with voters and bedecked with party favours. Many pedestrians not only wore party colours themselves but decorated their dogs too. By 7 o'clock in the evening when polling stopped, well over 90% of the electorate had voted. The ballot boxes were taken to Brunswick School for the count and Manchester Road was soon densely thronged with people. Some shopkeepers took the precaution of barricading their windows in case the crowd swayed into them.

(120 words)

If you feel yourself carried away with enthusiasm and you have the time, you can include many more details and have several paragraphs in each section. In this case you can call your sections 'chapters', and your project may well expand to something like 3,000 words.

3.   Remember the main elements of good historical writing: narrative and description together with explanation and analysis, and try to integrate them into your project, so that it is not simply a narrative account in chronological order. Be ready to ask questions: Why did that happen? Why did so-and-so act in the way he did? What were the results of his action? Why did the Liverpool railwaymen strike in 1911? If you can't find the answers in the documents, look at a secondary source (*see* end of this unit for suggestions). If you still fail to come up with an answer, don't worry too much; the fact that you are asking the questions shows that at least you are thinking in an historical way.

Try to interweave your explanations with the narrative, rather than keeping all the explanations to the end of the project.

All this may sound terribly difficult, but it can often be done quite briefly and simply. For instance, in a project about the strikes in the Nelson cotton mills in 1911, a student wrote:

The dispute reached a peak on 26 December when 18,000 weavers were on strike in Nelson and 45,000 looms were idle.

This is part of the narrative. He immediately goes on to give the explanation in the next paragraph:

The trouble was caused by the refusal of trade union members to work with non-unionists because the employers could get away with paying lower wages to non-unionists. Also small employers in outlying villages were not affiliated to the North East Lancashire Manufacturers' Association and again paid less than the Association rate. Thus, a weaver in Harle Syke (a village between Nelson and Burnley) was earning £6.10s a year less than a weaver doing the same work in a Burnley mill.

On the other hand, it would be equally possible when writing about such a topic as this to place the explanations first in a section of their own, as the writer of the Foulridge Church project did. (*see* p. 64)

4.   Try to relate what was happening locally to the national scene, to see whether the local area fitted in with the national pattern, or whether it was out of step with the rest of the country. This will not be possible for all topics, but it is a good feature if you can manage it, because it counters the common argument that local history has nothing to do with 'real' history which deals with the wider sweep of national events. In fact the best projects have shown that local studies can provide useful material to illustrate national trends. Strikes, trade unions and elections are well suited to this sort of treatment, though again you will have to look at a secondary source to find the necessary information.

Sometimes the link can be achieved briefly and without fuss: the writer of the Foulridge Church project, after explaining why a new Anglican church was needed in the village, remarks:

> There is strong evidence from all over the country that the Anglican church was losing its working-class flock to the Methodists. Building new Anglican churches was an attempt to win back the workers and steal a march on the Methodists.

Or you may decide to have a separate section – the conclusion of the Burnley election project was devoted to a brief examination of the national result. From a secondary source the writer discovered that the Liberals won a sweeping victory and she spent a couple of sentences explaining why the Conservatives fared so badly over the country as a whole.

5.   Be on the look-out for bias in your primary sources. This may show itself, for example, in comments in the Weavers' Union minutes about a mill-owner or in newspaper comments on the speeches of a parliamentary candidate. The *Burnley Express*, clearly sympathetic to the Conservatives, described some of the people who had voted Liberal or Socialist in 1906 as 'the more illiterate of the electors'. Be prepared to quote and comment on such titbits; this will show that you are aware of the pitfalls of primary sources.

Perhaps you will find your sources contradicting each other, as the author of the Fire Brigade project did. The Annual Report is full of praise for the speed and efficiency with which the brigade dealt with its first major fire in 1894; however, the *Colne and Nelson Times* complains sourly about the length of time the brigade took to arrive at the scene.

6.   Remember that you must not allow yourself to be too biased as you write up your findings. By all means reveal your point of view, but make sure that you consider both sides of the case. You may feel that the Harle Syke mill-owners were in the wrong in refusing to pay Association rates, and indeed you can point out that they were asking for trouble in the circumstances. What you should not do is to dismiss them as 'mean sods' as the writer of the project was tempted to do.

7.   The bulk of your information must come from a primary source or sources; secondary sources are to be used only for background or general information.

8.   Indicate, with dates, the primary source from which each major piece of information came. If yours is a short project based on one source, this is not important. All the information for the Burnley election was taken from two issues of the *Burnley Express*; here it is sufficient to mention at the end of the project the issues concerned. In a more complex one such as the Foulridge Church, drawn from a number of sources, you can show what came from where by using numbers in the text, which refer to a list at the end:
  1. *Colne and Nelson Times*, 14 May 1905
  2. Foulridge Church Magazine, January 1905
  3. Foundation Stone Laying Brochure
  4. Interview with Mrs Madge Emmott

and so on.

9.   You may include illustrations if you like; maps, sketches, photographs and photocopies can all add an extra dimension and bring colour and atmosphere to a project; for example, in the projects mentioned: photographs and plans of Foulridge Church, sketch maps of the village, one in 1842, one in 1905, showing how it had grown and changed; photographs of the candidates in the Burnley election and photocopies of handbills and advertisements – the list is endless.

Send your completed project to your tutor.

ASSIGNMENT E, OPTION II

THE ALTERNATIVE PROJECT BASED ON NEWSPAPERS

Choose one of the news items from the list that you made for Unit 5 and write a short piece about it (say, 500 words) mentioning

(a) the basic facts about what happened, as far as this is possible from the accounts in the different papers;
(b) the details about which the papers disagree;
(c) comments about possible reasons for the contradictions; these might include political bias, desire to present a sensational story, restrictions on reporting, confusion at the scene of a disaster and other special circumstances.
(d) comments about differences in style, vocabulary and presentation.

Don't hesitate to quote from the articles if you think this helps to illustrate your point.

If you decided to choose the Liverpool demolition story, your project might begin in this way:

> On May 16th 1982 the demolition contractors A. Ogden and Sons, blew up a number of blocks of derelict flats which had been standing empty for some months, at Kirkby, near Liverpool. Unfortunately, something went sadly wrong with the operation with the result that several nearby houses were destroyed, making their inhabitants homeless. The explosion also damaged a large number of other houses. Fortunately, nobody was injured because the contractors had evacuated all the houses in case a few windows were broken. These are the basic facts which most of the papers carrying the story (*Times, Guardian, Telegraph, Express* and *Mail*) seem to agree on. Oddly, neither the *Mirror* nor the *Sun* referred to the story at all.

This is an adequate opening paragraph, setting the scene but remaining uncontroversial. In your next paragraph you could go on to explain how the doubts and contradictions begin to creep in as you try to arrive at specific details:

> All five papers have extensive articles about the fiasco (the *Mail's* word for it), but when one begins to look beyond the basic facts for precise details, the job is not so easy. How many blocks of flats were demolished? A simple enough question one would have thought, but a precise answer is

not forthcoming. The *Guardian* states that four seven-storey blocks of flats were blown up 'with unexpected results'; the *Express* mentions 'five derelict tower blocks' and the *Telegraph* agrees. The *Times* seems to think only one block was brought down, while the *Mail* avoids mentioning the actual number but points out that the three remaining tower blocks will be pulled down in sections. Since the *Telegraph* says there were twelve blocks to begin with, does one then assume that nine had been demolished?

At this stage, with your two paragraphs, you have managed about 250 words – half way there! In your next paragraph you could describe other contradictions. Exactly how many other houses were destroyed? Again, there is no concensus. How many people were left homeless? How much was the damage valued at? Who would foot the bill?

As to the reasons for all these disagreements, one must assume that they were inevitable given the general confusion and chaos of the situation, though there seems no excuse for the *Times* being so far out of step with the others. Finally, in a concluding paragraph, you could write about differences in style and vocabulary, again quoting examples. Choices of headline are often revealing. In this particular story the *Express* used 'FURY OF BLAST FAMILIES' and talked about the demolition men having to take a blasting when they attended a public enquiry; 'the meeting lasted just 12 explosive minutes'. The reporter is here playing on words (punning) to introduce an element of wit and humour into the situation. You may feel that this approach is misplaced, but it is a common one in the 'popular' press. On the other hand, *The Times* and *The Guardian* report the incident soberly with no attempt to sensationalise.

I think you will find this exercise both enjoyable and revealing and you may well end up wondering how much of what you read in the papers you can accept without question.

Send your completed project to your tutor.

If you complete this unit successfully, whichever project you attempt, there is a good chance that the two main aims of the course mentioned in the Introduction will have been achieved: your interest in history will have been awakened or stimulated further, and your critical awareness will have been aroused. Best of all of course, you will have joined that select band of historians who have carried out a piece of original research!

SUGGESTED SECONDARY SOURCES THAT YOU CAN CONSULT:

Ayling, S. E., *The Georgian Century 1714-1837*, Harrap.
Ensor, R. C. K., *England 1870-1914*, Oxford.
Lowe, N., *Mastering Modern British History, 1815–Present Day*, Macmillan.
Mowat, C. L., *Britain Between the Wars, 1918-1940*, Methuen.
Peacock, H. L., *A History of Modern Britain, 1815-1968*, Heinemann.
Seaman, L. C. B., *Post-Victorian Britain, 1902-1951*, Methuen.
Taylor, A. J. P., *English History, 1914-1945*, Penguin.
Wood, A., *Nineteenth Century Britain*, Longman.
Woodward, E. L., *The Age of Reform, 1815-1870*. Oxford.

WHERE NEXT?

If you have enjoyed this course and feel you would like to take your study of history further, there are a number of options open to you.

SELF ASSESSMENT QUESTION

Firstly, it will be useful to think about which aspects of the course you enjoyed most, and about what you wish to get out of any further study.

		Tick
1.	*Did you most enjoy:*	
(a)	*doing the research;*	☐
(b)	*finding out about your own area;*	☐
(c)	*talking to other people about local history;*	☐
(d)	*reading secondary sources;*	☐
(e)	*writing about history in an academic way;*	☐
(f)	*finding out about national and international history?*	☐

		Tick
2.	*Would you most like to go on to:*	
(a)	*continue research;*	☐
(b)	*find out more about your locality;*	☐
(c)	*get an 'O' level;*	☐
(d)	*study events like the French Revolution?*	☐

If you ticked (a), (b) or (c) of (1) and (a) or (b) of (2), your interest is obviously primarily in doing practical local history. To take this further you could;

- ask in your local library whether a local history association or group exists in your area;
- try the NEC local history course (write for our *Guide to Courses*);
- read such books as *The Making of the English Landscape* by W. G. Hoskins (Penguin) or *The Making of your Neighbourhood* by Jack Ravensdale (BBC).

If you ticked (d), (e) or (f) of (1) and (c) or (d) of (2), your interest is obviously more academic, and you should consider;

- asking at your local Adult Education Centre whether they do an 'O' level at evening classes;
- taking the NEC 'O' level history course (write for our *Guide to Courses*);
- extending your own reading through your local library. You will find that as you read more history, you become increasingly interested in certain topics, and you may wish to read histories, biographies, etc. of particular events and people. Your librarian will always be pleased to suggest books you might like to try.

I hope this is helpful. In addition, NEC's student services department will always be pleased to offer advice, so do write to them. Whichever direction you choose, I hope this course has whetted your appetite for history, and that you will enjoy your future studies. Good luck!

COMMENTS ON THIS COURSE

We would like your comments on this course. Please send them to the Courses Editor, NEC, 18 Brooklands Avenue, Cambridge CB2 2HN.

Name. . . . .

Student No. . . . .

Address. . . . .

. . . .

. . . .

ED24